weir cooking

RECIPES FROM THE WINE COUNTRY

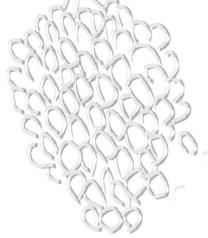

TIME
LIFE
BOOKS

TIME-LIFE BOOKS IS A DIVISION OF TIME LIFE INC.

TIME LIFE INC.
President and CEO   GEORGE ARTANDI

TIME-LIFE CUSTOM PUBLISHING
Vice President and Publisher   TERRY NEWELL
Vice President of Sales and Marketing   NEIL LEVIN
Director of Acquisitions   JENNIFER PEARCE
Editor   LINDA BELLAMY
Production Manager   CAROLYN CLARK
Quality Assurance Manager   JAMES D. KING

Produced by Chanticleer Press Inc.
Editor   ANN FFOLLIOTT
Designer   JIM WAGEMAN
Managing Editor   GEORGE SCOTT

Food photography by Richard Jung
Location photography by Bernie Schimbke
Illustrations by Jim Wageman, Wigwag

PRE-PRESS SERVICES, TIME-LIFE IMAGING CENTER
PRINTED IN CANADA.
10 9 8 7 6 5 4 3 2

TIME-LIFE IS A TRADEMARK OF TIME WARNER INC. U.S.A.

LIBRARY OF CONGRESS CATALOGING-IN-PUBLICATION DATA
WEIR, JOANNE.
    WEIR COOKING : RECIPES FROM THE WINE COUNTRY / BY JOANNE WEIR.
        P. CM.
    ISBN 0-7835-5327-7 (HARDCOVER)
    1. COOKERY, AMERICAN–CALIFORNIA STYLE.   I. TITLE.
    TX715.2.C34W45 1999
    641.59794–DC 21   99-17071
                    CIP

BOOKS PRODUCED BY TIME-LIFE CUSTOM PUBLISHING ARE AVAILABLE
AT A SPECIAL BULK DISCOUNT FOR PROMOTIONAL AND PREMIUM USE.
CUSTOM ADAPTATIONS CAN ALSO BE CREATED TO MEET YOUR SPECIFIC
MARKETING GOALS. CALL 1-800-323-5255.

weir cooking

RECIPES FROM THE WINE COUNTRY

Joanne Weir

Time-Life Books Alexandria, Virginia

Contents

CONTENTS

To my friend J.B., without whom Weir Cooking *would simply have been* Weir Cooked.

Acknowledgments

The very existence of this book and television series *Weir Cooking in the Wine Country* would not be possible without the generosity, support, and dedication of many talented people. First and foremost, I would like to thank my dear friend and producer, Linda Brandt, whose talent and vision continues to transcend my dreams. Her hard work, coupled with encouragement, paved a road I never thought I would venture along. From my heart, thank you for believing in me from the very beginning.

For their generosity and kind support, a special thanks goes to our funders, Calphalon, Beaulieu Vineyard (BV), and Peloponnese, as well as those individuals who donated their time, talent, furnishings and equipment to support this production.

My special thanks to Annie and Frank Farella of Farella Park Vineyards, who so graciously opened their home and continue to be a source of love, friendship and support. You're like family to me. And to Tom Farella, our unsung hero, for offering production support in ways that we couldn't even imagine.

To the entire television production team, whose expertise and professionalism are evident in each program you watch, I extend my heartfelt thanks: Bruce Franchini, Geof Drummond, Bernie Schimbke, Dean Gaskill, Mike Van Dine, Tim Bellen, Bill Bishop, Steve Bellen, Eliat Goldman, Pat Sielski, Nancy Bellen, Paul Swensen, Steve Siegelman, Terrance Ranger, Denise Vivaldo, John Bayless, Linda Jones, Bibby Gignilliat, Susan McKenna, Dean Carvalho, Angie Spensieri, Catharine Uyenoyama, Bernice, Chuck Fong, Cyrus Amini, Brian Sanders, David Sanborn, Leland Drummond, Helen Soehalim, Rob Weiner, Augie Cinquegrano, and Mike Elwell.

Special thanks to my brother, John Tenanes, for his time, love, and wonderful humor every day of my life. You're everything I could ever want in a big brother.

At Time-Life, I would like to thank my patient and talented editor, Linda Bellamy, who I know will join me for lunch one day. Thanks also to Terry Newell, Quentin McAndrew, Jennifer Pearce, Inger Forland, Neil Levin, and Ann ffolliott. Special thanks to Jim Wageman for designing such a lovely book.

To Richard Jung, I so appreciate your sensitivity and lovely photographs that grace the pages of this book. Thanks to food stylist Alison Attenborough for seeing food as I do. To Ivy and Michelle Syracuse, Carol Hacker, thank you. My heart goes out to Catherine Cogliandro Alioto, Jean Tenanes, Zoi Condos, Julie Rethmeyer, and Bernice Chuck Fong for their superb recipe testing and expertise. And to Steve Siegelman for all your time, for all of your thoughts, for all of your words.

To KQED in San Francisco, your support means more than I can express. Thanks to Peter Calabrese, DeAnne Hamilton, Regina Eisenberg, and Jolee Hoyt.

There are many farmers, growers, wine makers, and artisans who so generously shared their time and knowledge with both the book and the television series. The Wine Country of Northern California wouldn't be the culinarily rich and diverse land that it is without you. Thank you for your dedication and commitment in providing all of us with the best possible ingredients to cook with every day. Special thanks to Alice Waters, Christina Salas-Porras, Russell Moore and Gilbert Pilgram of Chez Panisse Restaurant, John Scharffenberger and Robert Steinberg of Scharffen Berger Chocolate Makers, Carlo and John Di Ruocco of Mr Espresso, Chad Robertson and Elisabeth Prueitt of Bay Village Bakers, Sue Connolly and Peggy Smith of Tomales Bay Foods, John Finger, Mike Watchorn, Terry Sawyer and James Tolbert of Hog Island Oyster Company, Steven Schack and Jennifer Bice of Redwood Hill Farms, Nan McEvoy and Tom Mainelli of McEvoy Ranch of Marin, Kirk and Carol Schmidt of Quail Mountain Herbs, Sally and Don Schmitt and Karen and Tim Bates of The Apple Farm, gardener John McRae, Thomas Webber of Seguin Moreau Napa Cooperage, Inc., Bruce and Ann Beekman of Beekman Apiaries, the California Artichoke Advisory Board, Nigel Walker of Eatwell Farm, Straus Family Creamer and Melissa's/World Variety Produce.

There are many people who offered advice and support with this project: Renée Behnke, Denise Bina, Jeff Cooley, Doralece Dulaghan, Gary Danko, Herb and Jane Dwight, Lisa Ekus, Priscilla Felton, Julie Hamilton, Ann Marie Howle, Ann Jenkins, Laurence Jossel, Sotiris and Lidia Kitrilakis, Natan Katzman, Mark Koppen, Paul Krapf, Sibella Kraus, Jill Kustner, Susanna Linse, Judy Lang, Chris Lee, Paul Angelo LoGiudice, Jennifer Louie, Tim McDonald, Sandy Musashi, Natalie Polin, Tosha Prysi, Jean Quan, Kathleen Rarey, Jerry Reid, Charlotte Robinson, Tina Salter, Shelley Sorani, Eric Spenske, Angel Stoyanof, Ned Takahashi, Alan Tangren, Chris Tracy, Karen Wang, and Hans Rathsack.

And of course, my thanks and love to Paulo for showing me the way.

The Wine Country: A Latitude and an Attitude

As strange as this may sound, my favorite places in the whole world are connected by a single straight line. It's the thirty-eighth parallel, and it runs right through all my spiritual homes: Sicily and Calabria in Italy, Murcia and Valencia in Spain, Athens in Greece, Izmir in Turkey—and, halfway around the globe—the earthly paradise known as the California Wine Country.

As a chef, cooking teacher, and food writer I get to travel all over the world. But the closer I stick to that good old thirty-eighth parallel, the happier I feel. And believe it or not, if I had to pick a single point on that line, I'd grab a sun hat and a picnic basket and head straight north across the Golden Gate to the Wine Country.

I've made that trip hundreds of times during the last few years as I researched this book and taped the 26-part television series to which it is a companion. I've gotten to know the wine country in all its seasons: the long hot days of summer, when the vines are green and heavy with grapes; the frenzied pace of the picking and crush in autumn; the quiet starkness of winter, and the magical return of spring, when the vineyards come alive with bright yellow mustard blossoms.

And the more I've seen of this amazing place, the more I'm struck by how it resembles the Mediterranean world, with its steeply sloping hills, intense sunlight, and vivid colors.

Those similarities weren't lost on the early European settlers of this region, who took what nature had to offer and remade it in the image of the world they had left behind, literally transplanting their roots in the rich, well-drained soil. They planted groves of olive and citrus trees, fruit and nut orchards, gardens filled with Mediterranean herbs and vegetables. And they discovered that the mild climate, with its arid summers, cool morning fog, bright, hot afternoons, and cooling Pacific breezes, was perfect for growing wine grapes.

A century-and-a-half later, California produces some of the greatest wines in the world. But don't let the term "wine country" fool you; grapes are just the beginning. The vineyards share their land with olive trees, sun-drenched fields, and gardens straight out of France, Italy, or Spain, brimming with a colorful "ratatouille" of sweet tomatoes ripening on the vine, juicy bulbs of garlic, red, green and yellow bell peppers, squash, and eggplant. Meyer lemon, fig, apple, Italian prune plum, persimmon, and walnut trees are everywhere, and the fragrance of rosemary, basil, wild fennel, thyme, lavender, and mint fill the air.

The California Wine Country is a beautiful, relaxing, inspiring place for anyone to visit. For a cook, it's heaven on earth. No wonder the whole "California Cuisine" movement—a bona fide food revolution that has changed the way

Americans cook and eat—began in the San Francisco Bay area, where the Wine Country is our backyard and the incredible bounty of Northern California is all around us.

I feel so lucky to have been a part of that movement. As a cook at Chez Panisse in Berkeley in the 1980s, I got to see how a handful of like-minded people—chefs, growers, foragers, and artisanal food producers—could show the whole world that no matter how modern and complex our lives become, the best food is still made from fresh, high-quality ingredients, grown and produced with respect for the land.

It's one thing to care about food. But these people and the generation that has followed them bring something more: a passion for finding the simple truths in what they do. They're growers who pioneer new or return to old sustainable agricultural practices and treat the land as a precious gift. They're cattle ranchers and oyster farmers, artisanal bakers and specialty coffee roasters. They're makers of olive oil, wine, cheese, and chocolate who have devoted their lives to mastering the old-world techniques of their craft that remind us all of a simpler way of life.

These are the people who inspired this book. Their spirit is what makes the Wine Country and Northern California so special, and I've tried to reflect that spirit in the recipes and reminiscences that follow.

So what is Wine Country Cooking? It's an un-fussy "New Mediterranean" style of preparing and eating food that changes with the seasons and celebrates the fruits of the field, the orchard, the pasture, the river, and the sea. It's also a lifestyle—a lifestyle in the slow lane with all the right priorities. It's taking an extra moment to really savor a great glass of wine or some vegetables you grew in your own garden. It's spending the whole afternoon cooking and catching up with family and friends. It's long, leisurely al fresco dinners with laughter and stories and big, bright platters of food that sparkle in the candlelight under a blanket of stars.

And, of course, it's a love of pairing food and wine to bring out the best qualities of both. Because in the Wine Country, as in the Mediterranean, people seldom drink without eating or eat without drinking. Wine isn't an afterthought, it's a part of everyday life. Wine is food.

And in that spirit, I urge you—if you're someone who worries about what food goes with what wine—to set aside what you've read or heard about the "rules" of food-and-wine pairing. Forget about "white with chicken, red with meat." Instead, think about how all the components of a dish go together. Say you're braising some chicken with olives. Syrah pairs beautifully with the assertive flavor of olives. Yes, a red wine with chicken!

Perhaps you've heard that salad can't be served with wine because of the acidity of the vinaigrette. Try a Sauvignon Blanc, which often makes a perfect complement to salad. Or experiment with reducing the acidity of the vinaigrette and adding a bit more oil. One of my favorite vinaigrettes, which is very wine-friendly, is made by boiling a cup of wine—Pinot Noir, Chardonnay and even Cabernet Sauvignon work well—until it is reduced to just a couple of tablespoons and has a syrupy consistency, then whisking in some fruity olive oil and a pinch of salt. Serve it with the same wine you used in the vinaigrette, and you'll be pleasantly surprised.

Here's a rule of thumb: the more a wine is oaked, the more difficult it is to pair it with food; oak dampens the fruitiness of wine and masks the flavor of food. I like wines with just a kiss of oak that let the freshness of the fruit and the brightness of the flavor shine through.

Salty and acidic foods decrease the acid perception of wine, making it taste sweeter. Sweet food has the opposite effect: wine tastes more acid and less sweet. Spicy foods bring out the tannins in wine, while rich, fatty foods decrease the perception of a wine's acidity and tannins. But the real rule is this: follow your nose and your taste buds, and enjoy what tastes good to you. Drink wines you like, and eat foods you like, and the rest will fall into place.

The same holds true for cooking. I'm always encouraging my students to experiment and try new things. Maybe it's mastering a new cooking technique. Or perhaps it's trying a new ingredient.

So go ahead. Throw caution to the winds and throw a little shaved fennel into that salad. While you're at it, why not try cooking a chicken under a brick? How about shucking some fresh fava beans—or maybe even growing some yourself? After all, how will you know what you might be missing unless you take a few chances every now and then? Keep things simple and focus on the goodness of the ingredients, and it will all work out.

That's how we do things in the Wine Country. And having cooked and eaten all over the planet, I can tell you that the Wine Country is more than just a part of the state of California. It's a state of mind: relaxed, refreshing, and festive, filled with lively flavors and brimming with possibilities. I hope this book gives you a taste of that happy state of mind and brings a world of delicious possibilities to your table.

The Olive

THE OLIVE

I've always wondered who "discovered" the olive. I mean, they grow on trees, of course. In fact, they're one of the oldest fruit trees known to man. But if you've ever tried eating one right off the tree, you know that this is some pretty strange fruit— unbearably astringent and bitter, like a cross between an unripe persimmon and an aspirin. So who had the imagination to say, "I know! Let's try curing these things for a few months and see if they shape up. Or maybe we could crush them and extract their oil"? Whoever it was, in my book, they're right up there with Columbus and Einstein.

Olives and olive oil are where cooking starts for me. A Chinese cook has soy sauce, a French cook has butter, but give me a decent olive oil and a handful of flavorful olives, and my mind starts racing. That's why I've devoted the first chapter of this book to the glories of the olive harvest.

Here in California, we've been harvesting olives for more than two hundred years. They arrived with the padres and were first planted in San Diego back in the late 1700s. Until fairly recently, the bulk of California olives have been table olives, but in the last decade, there's been a whole new wave of interest in California olive oil led by a band of pioneers like Nan Tucker McEvoy of McEvoy Ranch in Marin County. These growers are reviving traditional methods of cultivation and dreaming up new ones. They're importing root stock from Europe, and pressing small batches of olive oil that have begun, after much hard work, to rival the great oils of Italy, Spain, and Greece.

I like to think of it as our next gold rush— this time with liquid gold. It's exciting to watch. It reminds me of the 1960s, when the California Wine Country was transformed, in the hands of a few passionate visionaries like Robert Mondavi, into one of the great wine producing regions of the world. And it's happening in the very same places, as olive trees share the land with grapevines in more and more vineyards.

I found that out firsthand a few years ago, when I was living in the Napa Valley. I had a small house with an even smaller yard—nothing fancy. But if you sat looking out at the hills and vineyards, you could almost imagine you were in Tuscany or Catalonia—especially if the sun was setting and you were squinting. At the back of the yard was a small olive tree, and I spent a whole spring and summer watching it bear fruit. The olives were tiny—no bigger than a large pea. They looked a lot like the Elitses olives I'd seen on trips to Greece. I decided to try curing them. How hard could it be? People had been doing it for thousands of years. By late November, the olives had gone from green to black, and they were

Harvest

H A R V E S T

McEvoy Ranch in Marin County, California. Opposite: Olives ripening at McEvoy Ranch.

finally ripe. Bitter and hard as pebbles, yes, but ripe, a more expert friend assured me. I waited for the first break in the fall rains and, armed with a big basket and a stepladder, I picked and picked all afternoon until the tree was nearly bare and I was nearly paralyzed from stretching and twisting.

I rinsed my harvest in cool water. It was time to start curing. There are many techniques for curing olives. Somehow, I had settled on the most painstak-

Olives have been grown in California for more than two-hundred years.

ing of all: the tracking method. One by one, I placed the tiny olives on the stone steps behind my house and cracked them gently with a rock. An hour went by. Two hours. An entire afternoon. My hands turned black as tar.

When the cracking was done, I hauled out a huge earthenware bowl, poured in the olives and covered them with coarse salt and cold spring water as I'd seen people do all over the Mediterranean. The next day, I drained the olives, washed them under running water, and again covered them with salt

and water. And so it went for three more weeks. Each day, I'd taste the salt brine to see if the bitterness was gone. When the water was finally clear with no trace of bitterness, I drained the olives one last time, put them in glass jars, and covered them with fruity olive oil and pinches of crushed red pepper flakes. I ate those wonderful olives for a whole year, and each time I'd open a jar, I'd grin and give myself a little pat on the back.

Now, I'm not recommending that you take up olive curing—unless you have a great olive tree and a great deal of patience. To be honest, I was "cured" of the habit myself after that one attempt. But you can flavor them easily with oil and seasonings (see my recipe for Warm Olives with Fennel and Orange, page 14, for example), and you can use them to round out a dish and bring out the taste of other foods. Imagine the flavor of a few slabs of fresh tomato drizzled with some extra virgin olive oil, a few kalamata olives, some crumbled feta, and maybe a drizzle of balsamic vinegar, and you begin to see what I mean.

I use fruity, peppery, complex extra-virgin olive oils for dressings, pastas, and simple dishes in which its flavor can really shine through. "Pure" olive oil (usually a blend of refined and virgin oils) is fine for frying and with delicate foods that might be overpowered by a stronger-tasting oil.

One final word of advice: splurge! Buy the best olive oil you can get your hands on. Try a few of those specialty olives that are turning up in your grocery store. Keep tasting and experimenting. Like that first brave soul who ever tried an olive, you'll discover that one of the world's great treasures is right there under your nose.

Feta Preserved in Fruity Virgin Olive Oil with Summer Herbs

3 SPRIGS OF FRESH OREGANO

1 SPRIG OF FRESH ROSEMARY PLUS 2 SPRIGS AS A GARNISH

4 SPRIGS OF FRESH THYME

2 SPRIGS OF FRESH SAVORY (OPTIONAL)

$3/_4$ POUND (350G) FETA CHEESE

EXTRA-VIRGIN OLIVE OIL

$1^1/_2$ TEASPOONS CHOPPED FRESH OREGANO

$1/_2$ TEASPOON CHOPPED FRESH THYME

With the spine of a chef's knife, tap the herb sprigs gently to bruise the stems slightly.

Warm 1 cup (8 fl oz/250ml) of olive oil in a saucepan over medium heat. Add the oregano, rosemary, thyme, and savory sprigs and heat just until the herbs sizzle, 30 to 60 seconds. Remove from the heat and let cool.

Place half of the herbs and herb-scented oil in a 1-pint (500ml) Mason jar. Cut the feta to fit into the jar. Add the remaining herbs and oil to the jar. Add enough additional oil to cover the feta completely. Cover the jar and place in the refrigerator for a minimum of 2 weeks or up to 3 months.

To serve, bring the feta to room temperature and place on a platter. Discard the herb sprigs. Drizzle a few tablespoons of the oil over the cheese. Sprinkle with chopped fresh herbs, garnish with rosemary sprigs, and serve.

SERVES 6

There is nothing like the celebration of Greek Orthodox Easter. It starts the night before with a feast and concludes the next evening with another. A few years ago I spent the holiday on the island of Zakynthos, off the west coast of mainland Greece, where Maria Likouresis taught me how to preserve feta. She keeps it for months as it gets drier and more pungent. Try garnishing the platter with olives, roasted peppers, and caperberries. Don't forget a big basket of warm, crusty bread. Serve al fresco with drinks before dinner.

Warm Olives with Fennel and Orange

2 ORANGES
SALT
1 MEDIUM FENNEL BULB, CUT INTO EIGHTHS
$^3/_4$ CUP (6 FL OZ/185ML) EXTRA-VIRGIN OLIVE OIL
$^1/_2$ TEASPOON FENNEL SEED, COARSELY CRACKED
4 GARLIC CLOVES, PEELED AND THINLY SLICED
$^1/_8$ TEASPOON CRUSHED RED PEPPER FLAKES
4 OUNCES (120G) NIÇOISE OLIVES
4 OUNCES (120G) GREEN PICHOLINE OLIVES
2 OUNCES (60G) OIL-CURED OLIVES
2 OUNCES (60G) KALAMATA BLACK OLIVES

A glass of chilled champagne and a plate of warm olives studded with orange, fennel, and garlic is a perfect way to start any evening in the wine country. The briny, slightly salty flavor of the olives pairs well with a yeasty champagne or sparkling wine. Any leftovers? Place them in a Mason jar and store them in the refrigerator for up to a month. To serve, simply warm them gently.

With a vegetable peeler, remove 8 strips of orange peel, each 2-inches (5-cm) long. Try not to remove any of the white pith. If there is white pith, scrape it off with a paring knife.

Bring a large pot of salted water to a boil. Add the fresh fennel and cook for 3 minutes. Remove from the heat and drain.

Warm the olive oil in a large saucepan. Add the orange peel, fresh fennel, fennel seed, garlic, and red pepper flakes and cook until they begin to sizzle, about 1 minute. Add the olives and warm gently for 5 minutes. Remove from the heat and let sit 6 hours. Discard the orange peel.

Ten minutes before serving, warm the olives again. To serve, place the olives and fennel on a small platter. Drizzle with a few tablespoons of the oil and serve immediately.

SERVES 6

Feta and Olive Crostini

*S*o, you are grilling a butterflied leg of lamb for dinner. Here is a simple solution for what to serve while the lamb is on the grill. Try these crostini with a zippy topping of olives, feta, roasted red peppers, garlic, and mint. One recommendation—mix the topping ingredients together gently just before serving. This way the colors and flavors will stay vibrant and fresh.

1 LONG BAGUETTE, SLICED ON THE DIAGONAL INTO 24 $1/2$-INCH (1.25-CM) –THICK SLICES
2 TABLESPOONS EXTRA-VIRGIN OLIVE OIL
1 SMALL RED BELL PEPPER, ROASTED AND DICED (SEE PAGE 27)
1 GARLIC CLOVE, MINCED
2 TEASPOONS LEMON JUICE
1 CUP (6 OZ/180G) IMPORTED BLACK OLIVES, SUCH AS NIÇOISE OR KALAMATA, PITTED AND CHOPPED
2 TABLESPOONS CHOPPED FRESH FLAT-LEAF PARSLEY
$1^1/_2$ TABLESPOONS CHOPPED FRESH MINT
4 OUNCES (120G) FETA CHEESE

Preheat the oven to 400°F (200°C).

Brush both sides of the slices of bread lightly with olive oil. Place in a single layer on a baking sheet and bake, turning occasionally, until golden, 7 to 10 minutes.

In a bowl, mix together the red pepper, garlic, lemon juice, olives, parsley, and mint. Crumble the feta on top and mix gently just until combined.

Top each slice of bread with a tablespoon of the feta mixture and serve immediately.

MAKES 24 PIECES AND SERVES 8

Anchovy and Olive Crusts

8 ANCHOVY FILLETS (ABOUT 3 OZ/90G)

2 SHALLOTS, MINCED

1/2 CUP (3 OZ/90G) IMPORTED BLACK OLIVES, SUCH AS NIÇOISE
   OR KALAMATA, PITTED AND CHOPPED

3 TABLESPOONS EXTRA-VIRGIN OLIVE OIL

1 TABLESPOON RED WINE VINEGAR

4 GARLIC CLOVES, MINCED

1/4 CUP (1/4 OZ/7G) CHOPPED FRESH FLAT-LEAF PARSLEY

FRESHLY GROUND BLACK PEPPER

12 SLICES OF BAGUETTE, SLICED ON THE DIAGONAL INTO
   1/4-INCH (0.6CM) SLICES

LEMON WEDGES AS A GARNISH

WHOLE BABY RADISHES WITH THEIR TOPS AS A GARNISH

IMPORTED BLACK OLIVES AS A GARNISH

Place the anchovies in a bowl of cold water and soak for 10 minutes. Drain and pat dry with paper towels. Chop the anchovies and place in a bowl. Add the shallots, olives, and olive oil and stir together. Place the mixture on a cutting board and chop until the anchovies, shallots, and olives are very finely chopped. Return the mixture to the bowl. Add the vinegar, garlic, and parsley. Season to taste with pepper.

Toast the bread slices. Spread the anchovy and olive mixture on the toasts and broil just until warm, 30 to 60 seconds. Place the crusts on a platter and garnish with lemon wedges, radishes, and olives. Serve immediately.

Anchovies are a funny thing. You either love them or you hate them. This recipe is for any anchovy lover or anyone you may be trying to convert. I prefer to buy anchovies packed in salt rather than those packed in oil. They can be found in well-stocked markets with other bulk items such as olives, capers, and cornichons. The best method for ridding anchovies of a strong fishy flavor is to soak them in cold water for 10 minutes, then pat them dry with paper towels.

Crostini with Artichokes and Olives

6 WHOLE ARTICHOKES IN BRINE, VERY COARSELY CHOPPED

4 GRAPE LEAVES IN BRINE, STEMS REMOVED, RINSED, AND VERY
    COARSELY CHOPPED

$^1/_2$ CUP (3 OZ/90G) IMPORTED GREEN OLIVES, SUCH AS PICHOLINE, PITTED

1 GARLIC CLOVE, MINCED

$^1/_2$ TEASPOON GRATED LEMON ZEST

$1^1/_2$ TABLESPOONS EXTRA-VIRGIN OLIVE OIL

1 TABLESPOON LEMON JUICE

SALT AND FRESHLY GROUND BLACK PEPPER

1 LONG BAGUETTE, SLICED ON THE DIAGONAL INTO 16 $^1/_2$-INCH
    (1.25-CM) SLICES, TOASTED OR GRILLED

LEMON WEDGES AS A GARNISH

You can either cure your own artichokes or buy them already cured. To cure them yourself, pare them to the heart and stew them in a combination of olive oil, water, and lemon juice until tender. Combine them with grape leaves, olives, garlic, and lemon and spread on grilled or toasted bread. Serve with a glass of crisp Sauvignon Blanc.

In a bowl, combine the artichokes, grape leaves, olives, garlic, and lemon zest. Place on a cutting board and chop together until coarsely chopped. Return the mixture to the bowl and add the olive oil, lemon juice, and salt and pepper to taste.

To serve, spread the mixture onto the toasted bread and serve immediately, garnished with lemon wedges.

MAKES 16 PIECES AND SERVES 8

Rice "Olives"

2 TABLESPOONS EXTRA-VIRGIN OLIVE OIL
$1/2$ SMALL YELLOW ONION, MINCED
1 CUP (5 OZ/150G) ARBORIO RICE
$1 1/4$ CUPS (10 FL OZ/300ML) CHICKEN STOCK
$1 1/4$ CUPS (10 FL OZ/300ML) WHOLE MILK
$2/3$ CUP (6 OZ/180G) BLACK OLIVE PASTE (SEE NOTE)
SALT AND FRESHLY GROUND BLACK PEPPER
$1/4$ CUP (1 OZ/30G) FINELY GRATED PARMIGIANO REGGIANO CHEESE
1 CUP (4 OZ/120G) ALL-PURPOSE FLOUR
4 EGGS
4 CUPS (16 OZ/450G) TOASTED FRESH BREAD CRUMBS, FINELY GROUND
MIXTURE OF VEGETABLE AND OLIVE OIL, FOR FRYING

I bet you can't eat just one. I got this recipe from the Feron family, who grow rice in the Veneto region of Northern Italy. Gabrielle Feron likes to serve these bite-size antipasti—crisp on the outside and creamy inside—with drinks before dinner. As an alternative to olive paste, try using an equal amount of sun-dried tomato paste.

Heat the olive oil over medium heat in a skillet. Add the onions and sauté until soft, 7 minutes. Add the rice and continue to cook, stirring constantly, for 2 minutes.

Place the chicken broth and milk in a saucepan and heat just to a simmer. Immediately add to the rice mixture with half of the olive paste and salt and pepper. Bring to a simmer, reduce the heat to low, cover, and cook slowly until the rice is cooked, about 20 minutes. Add the remaining olive paste and the Parmigiano. Let cool completely.

Form the mixture into small olive-size balls using less than a tablespoon of mixture for each. Place the flour in a bowl. Whisk together the eggs and $1/2$ cup (4 fl oz/125 ml) water in another bowl. Place the bread crumbs in a third bowl. Roll the rice olives in the flour, then the egg, then the bread crumbs. Place on a baking sheet until you are ready to cook them.

Heat 1 inch of oil in a deep pan to 375°F (190°C). Fry the rice olives until golden on all sides, 60 to 90 seconds. Remove and serve immediately.

MAKES 60 BALLS, APPROXIMATELY 1 INCH (2.5CM) IN DIAMETER, AND SERVES 12

NOTE: OLIVE PASTE CAN BE PURCHASED FROM ANY WELL-STOCKED MARKET OR YOU CAN MAKE IT YOURSELF. PLACE PITTED KALAMATA OR NIÇOISE OLIVES IN THE FOOD PROCESSOR AND PULSE UNTIL YOU HAVE A COARSE PASTE.

Cannellini Bean Soup
with Rosemary Olive Oil

1$^1\!/_2$ CUPS (12 OZ/350G) DRIED WHITE NAVY OR CANNELLINI BEANS

4 TABLESPOONS (2 FL OZ/60ML) EXTRA-VIRGIN OLIVE OIL

1 MEDIUM YELLOW ONION, FINELY CHOPPED

1 CARROT, FINELY CHOPPED

1 CELERY STALK, FINELY CHOPPED

2 GARLIC CLOVES, MINCED

$^1\!/_2$ TEASPOON CHOPPED FRESH ROSEMARY

9 CUPS (72 FL OZ/2L) CHICKEN STOCK, VEGETABLE STOCK, OR WATER

1 RED BELL PEPPER, ROASTED, PEELED, AND DICED (SEE PAGE 27)

1 YELLOW BELL PEPPER, ROASTED, PEELED, AND DICED

$^1\!/_4$ CUP (1$^1\!/_2$ OZ/45G) IMPORTED BLACK OLIVES, PITTED AND DICED

1 TABLESPOON CHOPPED FRESH FLAT-LEAF PARSLEY

1 TABLESPOON RED WINE VINEGAR

SALT AND FRESHLY GROUND BLACK PEPPER

2 SPRIGS OF FRESH ROSEMARY

Perfect for a chilly evening, this soup is hearty enough to serve as a main course. All you need is a loaf of sourdough bread, a garden salad, and a bottle of Chianti to make it a meal. If time is precious, you can make the soup a few days ahead, and store it in the refrigerator until you are ready to heat and serve it.

Pick over the beans and discard any stones or damaged ones. Cover with water and soak for 4 hours or overnight.

Heat 1 tablespoon of the olive oil in a large soup pot over medium heat. Sauté the onions, carrots, and celery until soft, about 12 minutes. Add the garlic and chopped rosemary and continue to cook, stirring, for 2 minutes. Add the drained beans and stock or water, reduce the heat to low, and simmer slowly for 1 to 1$^1\!/_2$ hours.

In a small bowl, combine the red and yellow bell peppers, olives, parsley, red wine vinegar, and 1 tablespoon of the olive oil. Season to taste with salt and pepper, and reserve. With the spine of a chef's knife, tap the herb sprigs gently to bruise the stems slightly. Warm the remaining 2 tablespoons oil with the rosemary sprigs. As soon as it sizzles, remove from the heat and let cool for 1 hour. After 1 hour, strain the oil and discard the rosemary.

When the beans are tender, remove from the heat and let cool slightly. Puree one-third of the beans in the food processor or blender. Return the puree to the soup. Season to taste with salt and pepper.

Ladle the soup into bowls and drizzle with rosemary oil. In the center of each bowl, garnish with a spoonful of the chopped peppers and olives and serve immediately.

SERVES 6

Warm Olive and Caramelized Onion Tart

1 CUP (4 OZ/120G) ALL-PURPOSE FLOUR

$1/3$ CUP ($1^1/_4$ OZ/35G) CAKE FLOUR

SALT AND FRESHLY GROUND BLACK PEPPER

12 TABLESPOONS (6 OZ/180G) BUTTER, CUT INTO $1/_2$-INCH (1.25-CM) CUBES, FROZEN FOR 1 HOUR

3 TABLESPOONS ($1^1/_2$ FL OZ/45ML) EXTRA-VIRGIN OLIVE OIL

5 MEDIUM YELLOW ONIONS, THINLY SLICED (ABOUT $2^1/_2$ LB/1.2KG)

3 GARLIC CLOVES, CHOPPED

1 TEASPOON CHOPPED FRESH THYME

$1/_2$ TEASPOON CHOPPED FRESH ROSEMARY

1 CUP (8 OZ/240G)) PEELED, SEEDED, AND CHOPPED TOMATOES

2 ANCHOVY FILLETS, BONED AND SOAKED IN COLD WATER FOR 10 MINUTES, PATTED DRY, AND MASHED

$1/_2$ CUP (3 OZ/90G) IMPORTED BLACK OLIVES, PITTED AND COARSELY CHOPPED

*T*his free-form tart is a must when you have plenty of onions that you've pulled fresh from the vegetable garden. The simple pastry, made from ice-cold butter and flour in about 10 minutes, is a variation on labor-intensive puff pastry. After a 45-minute resting period, it's ready to use, a perfect foil for sweet or savory tarts.

Combine the 2 flours in a bowl and freeze for 1 hour. On a work surface, mix the frozen flour with $1/_2$ teaspoon salt. Add the cold butter and cut into $1/_4$-inch (6mm) pieces with a metal pastry scraper. Add ice water until the mixture almost holds together, up to $1/_4$ cup (2 fl oz/60ml).

Turn out onto a lightly floured board and press together as best you can to form a rough rectangular shape. There will be large chunks of butter showing. Work quickly and do not knead. Roll out the dough into a $1/_2$-inch (1.25-cm) –thick rectangle, about 5 x 7 inches. Fold the narrow ends toward the center to meet in the center. Fold in half again so that there are 4 layers. Turn the dough a quarter of a turn. This is your first turn. Roll again to form a rectangle $1/_2$-inch (1.25-cm) thick. Repeat the folding process. This is your second turn. Repeat the rolling and turning one more time. For the fourth turn, roll the dough and fold the dough into thirds as you would a business letter, wrap the dough in plastic wrap, and refrigerate for 45 to 60 minutes.

In the meantime, warm the oil in a skillet over medium-low heat. Add the onions, garlic, thyme, and rosemary, and cook over low heat, stirring occasionally, until the onions are soft and golden, 50 to 60 minutes. Add the tomatoes and continue to cook until almost dry, 10 to 15 minutes. Stir in the anchovies and olives, season to taste with salt and pepper, and set aside to cool.

Preheat an oven to 400°F (200°C). On a floured surface, roll the dough to a 13- x 9-inch (33 x 23-cm) rectangle, $1/_4$-inch (6mm) thick. Crimp the edges. Place the dough on a baking sheet. Cover the dough to within $1/_2$ inch (1.25 cm) of the edge with the onion mixture. Bake until the crust is golden and crisp, 30 to 40 minutes.

MAKES 1 RECTANGULAR TART, 13 x 9 INCHES (33 x 23 CM), AND SERVES 6

Warm Grilled Potato Salad
with Olives and Parmigiano Reggiano

$2^{1}/_{4}$ POUNDS (1KG) SMALL RED-SKINNED NEW POTATOES
5 TABLESPOONS (2 FL OZ/60ML) EXTRA-VIRGIN OLIVE OIL
SALT AND FRESHLY GROUND BLACK PEPPER
5 GREEN ONIONS, WHITE AND GREEN, THINLY SLICED
2 GARLIC CLOVES, MINCED
2 TABLESPOONS COARSELY CHOPPED FRESH FLAT-LEAF PARSLEY
2 TEASPOONS CHOPPED FRESH OREGANO
$^{1}/_{2}$ CUP (3 OZ/90G) IMPORTED BLACK OLIVES, PITTED
3-OUNCE (90-G) PIECE PARMIGIANO REGGIANO CHEESE

Preheat the oven to 375°F (190°C).

Wash the potatoes and place in a 13- x 9-inch (33- x 23-cm) baking dish. Drizzle with 1 tablespoon of the olive oil, season with salt and pepper, cover with foil, and bake until tender, 50 to 60 minutes.

Preheat an outdoor grill.

When the potatoes are tender and cool enough to handle, cut the potatoes in half. Place in a bowl and drizzle with 2 tablespoons of the olive oil. Grill, turning occasionally, until hot and golden, 5 to 7 minutes. Remove from the grill and place in a large serving bowl. Add the remaining 2 tablespoons olive oil, the green onions, garlic, parsley, oregano, and olives. Season to taste with salt and pepper. Using a cheese shaver, shave long thin pieces of Parmigiano Reggiano on top of the potatoes. Toss gently and serve immediately, while the potatoes are still warm.

SERVES 6

So, you've been a slave to the old-fashioned potato salad your mother used to make and serve at every family barbecue? Delicious, but you're ready for something a bit different. Try this one with potatoes hot and crisp from the grill, tossed with green onions, oregano, olives, and shaved Parmigiano. You won't go back, at least not for a while!

Tomato and Lemon Salad with Lemon-Scented Oil

3 LARGE LEMONS
$1/_4$ CUP (2 FL OZ/60ML) EXTRA-VIRGIN OLIVE OIL
$1^1/_2$ TABLESPOONS LEMON JUICE
1 SMALL SHALLOT, MINCED
SALT AND FRESHLY GROUND BLACK PEPPER
5 LARGE RIPE RED, YELLOW OR ORANGE TOMATOES,
    CUT INTO $^1/_2$-INCH (1.25-CM) SLICES
2 CUPS ($6^1/_2$ OZ/200G) COLORED CHERRY TOMATOES, HALVED
WHOLE LEAVES OF FLAT-LEAF PARSLEY AS A GARNISH

With a vegetable peeler, peel 2 of the lemons. Try not to remove any of the white pith. If there is white pith, scrape it off with a small paring knife.

Warm the olive oil in a saucepan over medium heat. Add the lemon peel and immediately remove the oil from the heat. Stir and set aside for 1 hour.

After 1 hour, strain the oil into a small bowl and discard the lemon peel. Add the lemon juice and shallots and whisk together. Season to taste with salt and pepper.

Slice the remaining lemon into paper-thin slices. To serve, place the sliced tomatoes and lemon slices on a serving platter, alternating the colors. Top with the cherry tomatoes and season with salt and pepper. Drizzle the vinaigrette over the tomatoes, garnish with lemon wedges and parsley leaves, and serve.

SERVES 6

Grilled Salad with Peppers, Olives, and Caperberries

4 LARGE RED BELL PEPPERS
4 LARGE YELLOW BELL PEPPERS
4 TABLESPOONS (2 FL OZ/60ML) EXTRA-VIRGIN OLIVE OIL
1 TABLESPOON RED WINE VINEGAR
1 TABLESPOON BALSAMIC VINEGAR
SALT AND FRESHLY GROUND BLACK PEPPER
$^1/_2$ CUP ($2^1/_2$ OZ/75G) CAPERBERRIES, ABOUT 20

*I*n some markets, you are faced with shelves of olive oil, sometimes 30 to 40 different varieties from a half dozen countries in varying grades. You will find inexpensive bottles of pure olive oil and special bottles of extra-virgin olive oil that will set you back one hundred dollars. And there are all kinds of flavored olive oils—lemon, tangerine, hot red pepper, porcini mushroom, garlic, even Tahitian lime. You can also make your own flavored oils. Here is a simple recipe for lemon-scented oil used with tomatoes.

1/2 CUP (3 OZ/90G) IMPORTED BLACK OLIVES, KALAMATA OR NIÇOISE

1 TEASPOON CHOPPED FRESH OREGANO

1/2 CUP (1/2 OZ/15G) LOOSELY PACKED WHOLE BASIL LEAVES

6 SLICES COARSE-TEXTURED COUNTRY-STYLE BREAD

2 WHOLE PEELED GARLIC CLOVES, SLICED IN HALF LENGTHWISE

Place the peppers directly on the gas jets or outdoor grill and char the peppers on all sides until the skins are completely black. Alternately, cut the bell peppers in half lengthwise and remove the stems, seeds, and ribs. Place cut side down on a baking sheet. Broil until the skins are black, 6 to 10 minutes. Transfer the peppers to a paper or plastic bag, close tightly, and let cool for 10 minutes. Remove the skins of the peppers by scraping with a knife. Cut the peppers into 1-inch-wide (2.5-cm-wide) strips and place in a bowl.

In another bowl, whisk together 3 tablespoons (1 1/2 fl oz/45ml) of the olive oil, the red wine vinegar, and balsamic vinegar. Season with salt and pepper. Add to the peppers and toss well. Place the peppers on a platter and sprinkle the caperberries, olives, oregano, and basil leaves on top.

Toast the bread until it is a light golden on each side. Rub the garlic clove lightly onto the surface of 1 side of the bread. Brush lightly with the remaining 1 tablespoon olive oil. Place the slices of toasted garlic bread around the edges of the salad and serve immediately.

SERVES 6

In the wine country, the weather is just right for serving many a dinner al fresco, and this simple, make-ahead salad is perfect. Olives and peppers marry well, whether with pasta, on a pizza, or in a salad. I have also added caperberries, available in well-stocked markets. If they are unavailable, substitute half the amount of capers.

Gold, at Its Best

WHEN I DROVE INTO TOWN, I could smell olives. I was in the village of Nyons, in the south of France, on a kind of food tour. I was quite young—not so young that we had backpacks, but with enough money to rent an Austin Mini. I had read in the guide books that Nyons was known for its olives and olive oil production.

This was several years ago, but I still remember seeing a bakery in the center of the village. Drawn to the window, I cupped my hands around my eyes to block out the sun, in order to see inside. There were shelves and shelves of all kinds of olive breads, in all shapes, colors, and sizes.

Just across the street, I looked up and saw a sign that read "Cooperative Agricole Huile d'Olives," a co-operative making olive oil. I followed the arrow, which took me about a mile out of town to a mill where an

old man was making olive oil.

It was harvest time and two young boys carried in a ton of olives wrapped in a large brown tarp. Immediately the olives were washed and placed in a large press that looked like a gigantic mortar and pestle. A bit of water was added into the mortar, then the pestle did the work of grinding the olives into a paste. Next, the olive paste was sandwiched between big hemp mats like rugs, called scourtins. Piled one on top of the other, the mats and paste were placed in a hydrolic press and, with pressure, the olive oil and water was forced out of the paste, down a trough, and into a wooden bucket. The water was ladled off and discarded, and the oil was pure gold.

I was given a taste. There began my lifelong addiction to fruity golden olive oil.

Orange, Avocado, and Green Picholine Olive Salad

2 LARGE NAVEL ORANGES

3 BLOOD ORANGES

3 TABLESPOONS ($1^1/_2$ FL OZ/45ML) ORANGE JUICE

1 TABLESPOON BALSAMIC VINEGAR

1 TEASPOON HONEY

3 TABLESPOONS ($1^1/_2$ FL OZ/45ML) EXTRA-VIRGIN OLIVE OIL

SALT AND FRESHLY GROUND BLACK PEPPER

2 MEDIUM RIPE AVOCADOS

$^3/_4$ CUP ($4^1/_2$ OZ/135G) GREEN PICHOLINE OLIVES, OR OTHER
    IMPORTED GREEN OR BLACK OLIVES

4 KUMQUATS, THINLY SLICED

FRESH CHERVIL AS A GARNISH, OPTIONAL

When the chill of winter is just beginning to thaw and give way to spring, it's the perfect time to make this colorful and flavorful salad. You'll find all kinds of citrus in the market, an ideal partner for creamy avocados and briny green picholine olives, native to the South of France.

Grate enough zest from 1 of the navel oranges to measure 1 teaspoon. Set aside in a small bowl. Using a sharp knife, cut the tops and bottoms off the navel and blood oranges to reveal the flesh. Cut off all of the peel so that no white pith remains. Cut the oranges crosswise into $^1/_4$-inch (6mm) slices. Set aside.

In the bowl containing the orange zest, whisk together the orange juice, balsamic vinegar, honey, and olive oil. Season to taste with salt and pepper.

When you are ready to assemble and serve the salad, cut the avocado in half from top to bottom. With a sharp knife blade, tap the avocado pit so that the blade lodges in the pit. Twist the knife slightly to remove the pit. Discard. With a large spoon, remove the flesh of the avocado in 1 piece. Cut each avocado half into 8 slices.

Place the various citrus slices on a serving plate, alternating with slices of avocado. Drizzle the vinaigrette over the oranges and avocado. Garnish with olives, kumquats, and chervil and serve immediately.

SERVES 6

Salad of Chick Peas, Olives, and Garden Herbs

1 CUP (7 OZ/210G) DRIED CHICK PEAS

$1/3$ CUP ($2^1/_2$ FL OZ/80ML) RED WINE VINEGAR

$1/3$ CUP ($2^1/_2$ FL OZ/80ML) EXTRA-VIRGIN OLIVE OIL

4 GARLIC CLOVES, MINCED

SALT AND FRESHLY GROUND BLACK PEPPER

2 TABLESPOONS CHOPPED FRESH BASIL

2 TABLESPOONS CHOPPED FRESH FLAT-LEAF PARSLEY

1 TABLESPOON CHOPPED FRESH MINT

2 TEASPOONS CHOPPED FRESH OREGANO

1 TEASPOON CHOPPED FRESH THYME

$1/_2$ TEASPOON CHOPPED FRESH ROSEMARY

$1/3$ CUP (2 OZ/60G) IMPORTED BLACK OLIVES, SUCH AS NIÇOISE OR KALAMATA, PITTED AND COARSELY CHOPPED

$1/3$ CUP (2 OZ/60G) IMPORTED GREEN OLIVES, SUCH AS PICHOLINE, PITTED AND COARSELY CHOPPED

4 GREEN ONIONS, WHITE AND GREEN, THINLY SLICED

HERB SPRIGS AS A GARNISH

Inspired by the sunny South of France, I tossed chick peas with cured green and black olives, fruity olive oil, plenty of garlic, and all kinds of herbs from my summer garden. Serve with grilled fresh tuna steaks or skewers of chicken. The chick peas can be cooked a few days in advance. Add the vinegar and oil while they are still warm and store in the refrigerator. Bring to room temperature before adding the remaining ingredients.

Pick over the chick peas and discard any stones or damaged ones. Cover with water and soak for 4 hours or overnight.

Place the chick peas in a saucepan with plenty of water. Simmer uncovered until the skins begin to crack and the peas are tender, 50 to 60 minutes. Drain.

In a large bowl, whisk together the vinegar, olive oil, and garlic. Season to taste with salt and pepper. Add the chick peas and let cool.

Add the chopped parsley, basil, mint, oregano, thyme, rosemary, olives, and green onions and toss well. Season to taste with additional salt and pepper, if needed. Place in a serving bowl, garnish with herb sprigs, and serve.

SERVES 6

Penne with Olio Santo, Ricotta Salata, Olives, and Mint

1/4 CUP (2 FL OZ/60ML) EXTRA-VIRGIN OLIVE OIL

1/2 TEASPOON CRUSHED RED PEPPER FLAKES OR 2 DRIED
        HOT RED CHILIES, CRUMBLED

2 CUPS (16 FL OZ/475ML) CHICKEN STOCK

12 OUNCES (350G) DRY PENNE OR FUSILLI PASTA

1/2 POUND (225G) RICOTTA SALATA CHEESE, CRUMBLED

3/4 CUP (41/2 OZ/135G) IMPORTED BLACK OLIVES, PITTED
    AND COARSELY CHOPPED

SALT AND FRESHLY GROUND BLACK PEPPER

3 TABLESPOONS (1/4 OZ/8G) CHOPPED FRESH MINT

To make olio santo, heat the olive oil in a saucepan over medium heat until warm. Add the red pepper flakes, remove from the heat immediately, and let sit for 2 hours. Strain and discard the pepper.

In the meantime, bring the chicken stock to a boil and reduce until 3/4 cup (6 fl oz/180ml) remains. Reserve.

Bring a large pot of salted water to a boil. Add the pasta and cook until al dente, 8 to 10 minutes or according to the directions on the package. Drain and immediately return to the pot. Add the reduced chicken stock, olio santo, ricotta salata, and olives. Toss together and season to taste with salt and pepper. Place in a serving bowl and sprinkle with mint. Serve immediately

SERVES 6

*O*lio santo, or saint's oil, is a favorite condiment made in Italy. Spicy hot dried red peppers are added with abandon to fruity virgin olive oil. Usually olio santo is added just before serving the finished recipe, to give a bit of a zap to any dish. It certainly does the trick here.

Some people believe in retail therapy. When the going gets tough, they go shopping. But buying a new pair of shoes doesn't do it for me. When I'm feeling stressed out or a little blue, I get out my big canvas bag and head straight for the nearest farmer's market. There's nothing like a market to bring me back down to earth and give my spirits a lift. I always know I'll bump into a friend or two—a grower, a fellow food writer, a chef—and I love to poke around and see what's in season. Just seeing and smelling all those beautiful fresh fruits and vegetables, artisanal cheeses and breads, and dazzling flowers wakes up my brain and makes me want to go home and get cooking.

We're really lucky in Northern California because we're right in the middle of a small-farming revolution. Independent growers, many with just a few acres of land, are proving that even in the face of agribusiness and real estate development, specialty farms—often run by single families—are alive and well. It's not an easy life, of course. It takes hard work, 24-hour-a-day dedication, and, with the surprises nature deals you, a healthy love of gambling. But for all that, the movement is gaining momentum.

I remember how it began back in the late 1970s, when restaurants like Chez Panisse began working with local growers to provide high-quality, carefully grown produce and specialty items for their kitchens. Back then, there were hardly any farmer's markets around here. In the urban areas, chefs were about the only people who had access to produce grown on small farms. But as their customers began to taste how wonderful California produce could be, consumer demand started to grow.

Today, there are some fifty farmer's markets in the San Francisco Bay Area alone, and for many of the farmers who sell there, these markets are the life-line that's kept them in business. They can get higher profit margins by selling directly to consumers rather than just to retailers or wholesalers. And consumers, meanwhile, still find their prices and selection to be some of the best around.

But it's more than prices and the selection that brings me back to the Ferry Plaza Farmer's Market in San Francisco every week. It's the people. It's the nectarine lady saying with a friendly wink, "If you think these are good, wait till next week!" It's the date guy telling me his recipe for "date shakes" made in

THE GARDEN

from the Garden

The first tomatoes of the season are eagerly anticipated
by gardeners and cooks across North America.

Joanne selects fresh tomatoes at the San Francisco farmer's market.

the blender with his sweet, rich, vanilla-scented Barhi dates. It's my old friend Joe Minocchi of White Crane Springs Ranch bringing me homegrown lemon verbena and myrtle for my elixirs. Or Sue Conley from Cowgirl Creamery handing me a spoonful of her crème fraîche with an enthusiastic "Check this out. It just won a first prize from the National Cheese Society!"

If there's a farmer's market anywhere near you, I encourage you to set aside a few hours and plan a field trip. Bring a large bag with shoulder straps to hold your treasures. Arrive early—the good stuff always sells out fast. And start with a quick tour of the whole place before you buy, so you can scope out the best sources for everything. Don't be shy about asking for tastes and chatting about what's for sale. That's the most fun of all! You'll be amazed at how much there is to learn about the food you eat, and you'll probably get some free cooking advice while you're at it.

These days, it seems like you can get just about any kind of produce all year in most major grocery stores. Even in December, somebody, somewhere in the world is growing cherries and shipping them to the United States. But farmer's markets put us all back in touch with what's in season right now, right where we are. You don't have to wonder if an ear of corn that looks beautiful will have any flavor. What you see is what's fresh and good, often picked that very morning.

It's a year-round floor show, and there's never a dull moment. Winter brings colorful squashes, robust greens, hearty root vegetables, and wild mushrooms. In the spring, the market is filled with green as lettuces, pea shoots, tender asparagus, baby vegetables, green garlic, and green onions come into their own. Then comes summertime, and the cooking is easy, because the fabulous vegetables and fruits of the season need only the simplest preparations. There are vine-ripened heirloom tomatoes, corn on the cob, sweet bell peppers, summer squashes, green beans, and all kinds of fresh herbs to sprinkle over them. As the days grow shorter and the sun more scarce, the market becomes a golden cornucopia of earthy fall vegetables: pumpkins, hard-shelled squashes of every kind, mushrooms, and root vegetables. It's time to go home, make soup, and wait for the whole remarkable cycle to begin again.

Ever since I moved into San Francisco, I've missed the thrill of stepping out into the garden and "picking up a few things for dinner." Luckily, the farmer's market is always there, week after week, like an old friend, reminding me that a garden isn't just the little patch of land behind your house. If you know where to look, the delights of the garden are yours for the gathering all year long.

Golden Gazpacho with Garlic Croutons

4 POUNDS (1.8KG) FRESH RIPE YELLOW TOMATOES, PEELED, SEEDED,
   AND CHOPPED
1 YELLOW OR GREEN BELL PEPPER, SEEDED AND COARSELY CHOPPED
1 MEDIUM RED ONION, COARSELY CHOPPED
1 LARGE CUCUMBER, PEELED, HALVED, SEEDED, COARSELY CHOPPED
6 TABLESPOONS (3 FL OZ/90ML) RED WINE VINEGAR
3 LARGE GARLIC CLOVES, MINCED
3 TABLESPOONS (1 1/2 FL OZ/45ML) EXTRA-VIRGIN OLIVE OIL
1 SLICE COARSE-TEXTURED COUNTRY-STYLE BREAD, CRUSTS REMOVED,
   SOAKED IN WATER, AND SQUEEZED DRY
SALT AND FRESHLY GROUND BLACK PEPPER

FOR THE GARNISH
2 TABLESPOONS EXTRA-VIRGIN OLIVE OIL
3 GARLIC CLOVES, PEELED AND CRUSHED
6 SLICES WHITE BREAD, CRUSTS REMOVED, CUT INTO SMALL CUBES
1/4 CUP (1 OZ/30G) DICED GREEN BELL PEPPER
1/4 CUP (1 OZ/30G) PEELED, SEEDED, AND CHOPPED CUCUMBER
1 1/2 CUPS (8 OZ/240G) RED CHERRY TOMATOES, QUARTERED
1/4 CUP (1 1/2 OZ/45G) DICED RED ONION

In a bowl, mix the tomatoes, bell pepper, onions, cucumber, vinegar, garlic, olive oil, and bread. In batches, puree the soup in a blender on high speed, about 3 minutes per batch, until very smooth. Strain through a coarse strainer into a large bowl. Season with salt and pepper, place in the refrigerator, and chill for 1 hour.

For the garnish, warm the olive oil in a skillet over medium heat. Add the crushed garlic and cook until the garlic is golden brown, about 1 minute. Remove the garlic and discard. Add the bread cubes and stir to coat with olive oil. Cook slowly, stirring occasionally, until bread cubes are golden, 10 to 12 minutes.

To serve, ladle the chilled soup into bowls and garnish with the bell peppers, cucumbers, tomatoes, red onion, and croutons. Serve immediately.

SERVES 6

Native to Spain, where summers are blazing hot, this chilled liquid-salad soup brings relief to the parched. And here in North America, from Atlantic City to Santa Barbara, wherever there is the smallest patch of soil or sunny corner, you will find tomatoes growing during the summer. They get canned, frozen, squeezed, sliced, oven-dried, and stewed. For this ice-cold soup, use your ripest tomatoes picked fresh from the garden. If yellow tomatoes are unavailable, substitute ripe red ones.

Oven-Roasted Beet Soup with Watercress

2½ POUNDS (1.1KG) BEETS, GREENS REMOVED AND WASHED
2 TABLESPOONS EXTRA-VIRGIN OLIVE OIL
SALT AND FRESHLY GROUND BLACK PEPPER
1 LARGE RED ONION, MINCED
5 CUPS (40 FL OZ/1.1L) CHICKEN STOCK
1 BUNCH WATERCRESS, STEMS REMOVED, CHOPPED
½ CUP (4 FL OZ/120ML) CRÈME FRAÎCHE
1 TEASPOON LEMON JUICE

I love beets, but I don't think there is any vegetable that is more maligned. Beets don't deserve it! I think it comes from all those mothers in the 1950s who boiled beets and threw the flavor out with the water. After being boiled in water, the only flavor left in the beets is like the dirt they are grown in. Instead, my favorite way to cook them is to roast them in the oven, which accentuates their sweetness. Honestly, I promise you'll like them.

Preheat the oven to 375°F (190°C).

Place the beets in a shallow baking pan and drizzle with the oil and 1 tablespoon water. Roll the beets to coat with the oil. Season with salt and pepper, cover with aluminum foil, and bake until the beets are tender and can be easily pierced with a fork, 60 to 80 minutes, depending on the size of the beets. When the beets are tender, remove from the oven and let cool. This can be done a day in advance.

In the meantime, pour the oil from the baking pan into a soup pot. Warm the oil over medium heat, add the onions, and cook, stirring occasionally, until soft, about 7 minutes.

When the beets are cool enough to handle, peel and chop them coarsely. Add them to the onions along with the chicken stock and 1 cup water. Increase the heat to high and bring to a boil. Reduce the heat to low and simmer for 20 minutes. Let cool for 10 minutes.

In batches, puree the soup in a blender on high speed, 3 minutes per batch, until very smooth. Strain through a fine mesh strainer into a clean soup pot. Season to taste with salt and pepper.

Reserve ¼ cup of the watercress for a garnish. In the blender, puree half of the watercress with 1 tablespoon crème fraîche until very smooth. Add the remaining watercress and pulse 2 to 3 times. Add lemon juice and season to taste with salt and pepper.

SERVES 6

Harvest Vegetable Soup with Pesto

$^1/_2$ CUP (3$^1/_2$ OZ/100G) DRIED CANNELLINI BEANS

6 TABLESPOONS (3 FL OZ/90ML) EXTRA-VIRGIN OLIVE OIL

1 SMALL YELLOW ONION, CHOPPED

2 SMALL CARROTS, PEELED AND CUT INTO $^1/_2$-INCH (1.25-CM) DICE

2 SMALL CELERY STALKS, CUT INTO $^1/_2$-INCH (1.25-CM) DICE

2 CUPS (12 OZ/350G) PEELED, SEEDED, AND CHOPPED TOMATOES

4 CUPS (32 FL OZ/900ML) CHICKEN STOCK

$^1/_2$ PACKED CUP (1$^1/_2$ OZ/45G) FRESH BASIL LEAVES, WASHED AND DRIED

1 TABLESPOON TOASTED PINE NUTS (SEE PAGE 42)

1 GARLIC CLOVE, MINCED

1 CUP (4 OZ/120G) GRATED Parmigiano Reggiano CHEESE

SALT AND FRESHLY GROUND BLACK PEPPER

$^1/_2$ POUND (225G) GREEN BEANS, ENDS TRIMMED AND CUT INTO
    1-INCH (2.5-CM) LENGTHS DIAGONALLY

$^1/_4$ POUND (120G) FUSILLI PASTA

3 CUPS (1 LB/450G) LIGHTLY PACKED Swiss chard LEAVES,
    1 SMALL BUNCH, CUT INTO 1-INCH (2.5-CM) PIECES

Is there any better sight than a garden full of fresh vegetables? This is the time to grab a basket and pick whatever you'd like to make a fresh vegetable soup, which is a meal on its own. Spoon some of the sweet basil pesto into the soup just before serving. This is the best part; be sure to pass the rest of the pesto so your guests can help themselves to more at the table.

Pick over the cannellini beans and discard any stones or damaged ones. Soak the beans in cold water for 4 hours or overnight. Drain the beans and place them in a large saucepan with plenty of water. Simmer uncovered until the beans are tender, 45 to 60 minutes. Drain the beans.

Heat 2 tablespoons of the olive oil in a large soup pot over medium-low heat. Add the onions, carrots, and celery and cook, stirring occasionally, until the vegetables are tender, 20 minutes. Add the tomatoes, stock, and 3 cups (24 fl oz/750ml) water and simmer until the vegetables are tender, about 45 minutes.

In the meantime, place the basil, pine nuts, garlic, the remaining 4 tablespoons (2 fl oz/60ml) olive oil, and $^1/_2$ cup (2 oz/60g) of the Parmigiano in a blender or food processor. Blend at high speed until well mixed, about 1 minute. Stop and scrape down the sides periodically and continue to blend until smooth. Season with salt and pepper.

Fifteen minutes before serving, add the cooked cannellini beans, green beans, and pasta and simmer, covered, until the pasta is completely cooked, 8 to 10 minutes. Add the Swiss chard and simmer until it wilts, about 5 minutes. Season with salt and pepper.

Ladle the soup into bowls, top with a large spoonful of pesto, sprinkle with the remaining $^1/_2$ cup (2 oz/60g) Parmigiano, and serve.

SERVES 6

Asparagus Soup with Lemon Crème Fraîche

3 POUNDS (1.4KG) ASPARAGUS, ENDS REMOVED AND DISCARDED

2 TABLESPOONS UNSALTED BUTTER

1 ONION, CHOPPED COARSELY

6 CUPS (48 FL OZ/1.4L) CHICKEN STOCK

2 TABLESPOONS (1 FL OZ/30ML) LEMON JUICE

SALT AND FRESHLY GROUND BLACK PEPPER

$^1/_2$ CUP (4 FL OZ/120ML) CRÈME FRAÎCHE

1 TEASPOON GRATED LEMON ZEST

Along with the crocuses, jonquils, and budding grapevines, the first green tips of asparagus poking their heads from the spring soil is a sign that warm weather is just around the corner. This asparagus soup heralds the awakening of spring with a light lift of lemon-scented crème fraîche.

Slice off 1 inch (2.5cm) of the asparagus tips. Slice them diagonally into thin slivers. Reserve. Cut the remaining asparagus roughly into 3/4-inch (2-cm) lengths. Reserve separately.

Melt the butter in a soup pot over medium heat. Add the onions and cook, stirring occasionally, until soft, about 7 minutes. Add the 3/4-inch (2-cm) lengths of asparagus and the chicken stock. Bring to a boil over high heat, reduce the heat, and simmer until the asparagus is tender, about 12 minutes. Let the soup cool for 15 minutes. In batches, puree the soup in a blender on high speed, 3 minutes per batch, until very smooth. Strain through a fine mesh strainer into a clean soup pot. Season to taste with salt and pepper. Add 1 tablespoon of the lemon juice and season with salt and pepper. Add additional water to correct the consistency if the soup is too thick.

In a bowl, mix together the crème fraîche, lemon zest, remaining 1 tablespoon lemon juice, and salt and pepper. Add 1 to 2 tablespoons of water to thin slightly to make a pourable consistency.

To serve, bring the soup to a simmer over medium heat. Add the asparagus tips to the hot soup and simmer slowly until the asparagus tips are tender, 2 to 3 minutes. Ladle the soup into bowls. Drizzle with the lemon crème fraîche and serve immediately.

SERVES 6

Grilled Corn and Arugula Salad
with Smoked Tomato Vinaigrette

3 EARS FRESH CORN, IN THEIR HUSKS

2 RED BELL PEPPERS

1 TOMATO, DICED

$1/_2$ GARLIC CLOVE, CHOPPED

1 TABLESPOON RED WINE VINEGAR

$1/_4$ CUP (2 FL OZ/60ML) EXTRA-VIRGIN OLIVE OIL

SALT AND FRESHLY GROUND BLACK PEPPER

3 BUNCHES ARUGULA, STEMS REMOVED, ABOUT 8 CUPS (1 LB/450G)

$3/_4$ CUP ($4^1/_2$ OZ/135G) IMPORTED BLACK OR GREEN OLIVES

$1^1/_2$ CUPS (8 OZ/240G) RED AND YELLOW CHERRY TOMATOES, HALVED

3-OUNCE (90G) PIECE OF PARMIGIANO REGGIANO CHEESE

Prepare a charcoal grill.

Grill the corn and peppers 4 inches (10cm) from the coals, turning occasionally, until the skins of the peppers are black, the corn husks are black, and the corn kernels are light golden when the husk is pulled back, 6 to 10 minutes. Remove from the grill and transfer the peppers to a paper or plastic bag, close tightly, and let cool for 10 minutes. Let the corn cool.

Remove the husks and silk. Cut the kernels from the cob and set aside. Scrape the skin from the pepper with a knife. Reserve separately.

In a blender, puree the pepper, tomato, garlic, vinegar, and olive oil. Season with salt and pepper, strain through a fine mesh strainer, and reserve.

On individual serving plates, divide the vinaigrette evenly among the plates. In a large bowl, toss together the corn and arugula and distribute onto the plates. Garnish with olives and cherry tomatoes. Shave the Parmigiano over the top. Serve immediately.

SERVES 6

Corn on the cob has far too short a season. So when it's fresh and sweet, roast it with bell peppers on a charcoal grill. Use the peppers with tomatoes to make a slightly smoky vinaigrette to toss with peppery arugula, corn kernels, Parmigiano, olives, and cherry tomatoes, a combination inspired by my friend the chef Gary Danko. Your efforts will be well worth it.

Corn for Sale

WHEN I WAS GROWING UP in New England, we waited for the first ear of corn to be picked with such anticipation, like that last day of school before summer vacation.

When my grandfather picked the first corn of the season, my grandmother would have the water boiling as he came into the kitchen, his arms loaded. I'd watch him sit in a chair, lean over a paper bag, and husk the corn, dropping the husks and silk directly into the bag.

He carefully piled up the corn, as if it were gold bullion.

My grandmother would add a fistful of salt to the water and then, one by one, drop the ears of corn into the water. After about four or five minutes, out they'd come. She would set a big platter of corn in the center of the table and we would make a meal of just home-made butter and fresh corn. My grandmother's butter was saltier than most, and this was the only time she'd let us run the corn along the butter, making a groove in it that perfectly matched the kernels of corn.

Height-of-Summer Five Tomato Salad with Gorgonzola Toasts

When I was a kid, I remember going to the grocery store and seeing four hard, pink tomatoes all lined up and packed in a plastic basket, then covered with cellophane. We've come a long way! Now, at the height of summer, freshly pickled vine-ripened tomatoes from the garden or a selection of heirloom tomatoes from the local farmer's market bear almost no resemblance to the hard, pink tomatoes of my youth.

3 TABLESPOONS (1 OZ/30G) PINE NUTS

2 TABLESPOONS UNSALTED BUTTER, AT ROOM TEMPERATURE

3 OUNCES (90G) GORGONZOLA CHEESE, AT ROOM TEMPERATURE

3 TABLESPOONS (1^1/$_2$ FL OZ/45ML) EXTRA-VIRGIN OLIVE OIL

3 TABLESPOONS (1^1/$_2$ FL OZ/45ML) BALSAMIC VINEGAR

1 TABLESPOON HONEY

SALT AND FRESHLY GROUND BLACK PEPPER

2 LARGE RIPE YELLOW TOMATOES, CUT INTO ^{1}/$_2$-INCH (1.25-CM) SLICES

3 LARGE RIPE RED TOMATOES, CUT INTO ^{1}/$_2$-INCH (1.25-CM) SLICES

2 LARGE RIPE ORANGE TOMATOES, CUT INTO ^{1}/$_2$-INCH (1.25-CM) SLICES

3 MEDIUM ZEBRA STRIPE OR OTHER HEIRLOOM TOMATOES, CUT INTO ^{1}/$_2$-INCH (1.25-CM) SLICES

^{1}/$_2$ POUND (240G) ASSORTED COLORED CHERRY TOMATOES, HALVED

6 SLICES COARSE-TEXTURED COUNTRY-STYLE BREAD, TOASTED

3 TABLESPOONS (^{1}/$_2$ OZ/15G) FINELY SNIPPED CHIVES

Warm a skillet over medium high heat. Add the pine nuts and cook, stirring constantly, until golden, 1 to 2 minutes. Remove from the pan and let cool. Place in a bowl with the butter and Gorgonzola and mash together with a fork.

In a small bowl, whisk together the olive oil, vinegar, and honey. Season to taste with salt and pepper.

Preheat the oven to 400°F (200°C). Ten minutes before serving,

You Say Tomato

THERE IS HARDLY A summertime pleasure greater than taking your first bite of a ripe, juicy red tomato fresh off the vine. The garden tomato has survived multiple names, transformations, disingenuous descriptions, and a long migration from the New World to the rest of the world and back, to become one of the most popular foods in American cuisine. Not only do we like to eat tomatoes, but between 25 to 40 million of us love to grow hundreds of varieties in gardens, containers, and window boxes. There's a tomato for just about every personality, space, and climate. Even I have a few trellised tomato plants. They are cherry tomatoes, but still I manage to make a few tomato salads with them.

More than any other fruit or vegetable, the tomato has changed the face of modern cuisine. Most of us have at least a few cans of tomatoes in the pantry. And no matter where we live, we look forward to growing our own tomatoes or buying them fresh at the farmers' markets. No other fruit or vegetable is anticipated with such enthusiasm.

alternate the slices of tomato on a serving plate. Sprinkle the cherry tomatoes over them. Season to taste with salt and pepper. Drizzle with the vinaigrette.

Spread the cheese mixture on the toasted bread. Place the bread on a baking sheet and bake on the top shelf of the oven until the bread is golden brown around the edges, 1 to 2 minutes. Cut the bread on the diagonal into 3-inch (7.5cm) pieces. Place the Gorgonzola toasts around the edges of the serving plate. Sprinkle the top of the salad and toasts with chives and serve immediately.

SERVES 6

Asparagus, Blood Orange, and Prosciutto Salad

4 BLOOD ORANGES
$1/_4$ CUP (2 FL OZ/60ML) BLOOD ORANGE JUICE
2 TABLESPOONS WHITE WINE VINEGAR
$1/_4$ CUP (2 FL OZ/60ML) EXTRA-VIRGIN OLIVE OIL
SALT AND FRESHLY GROUND BLACK PEPPER
2 POUNDS (1.8KG) FRESH ASPARAGUS, LARGE SPEARS, ENDS SNAPPED OFF
12 THIN SLICES PROSCIUTTO, EACH CUT INTO 2 PIECES THE LONG WAY

Grate enough zest from 1 of the blood oranges to measure 1 teaspoon. Set aside in a small bowl. Using a sharp knife, cut the tops and bottoms off the oranges to reveal the flesh. Cut off all of the peel so that no white pith remains. Cut the oranges into sections between the membranes. Discard any seeds. Set aside in a separate bowl.

In the bowl containing the orange zest, whisk together the orange juice, vinegar, and olive oil. Season to taste with salt and pepper.

Bring a large, shallow pan of salted water to a boil. Add the asparagus and cook until just tender, 4 to 6 minutes. Remove from the water. Place in a single layer on a serving platter and cool in the refrigerator.

When the asparagus is cool, scatter the orange sections over the asparagus. Drizzle with the vinaigrette. Place the prosciutto strips like curled ribbons over the top of the salad and serve.

SERVES 6

As soon as the weather starts to warm up, you can kiss asparagus good-bye. Asparagus and blood oranges love the coolness of spring. Add a few thin slices of prosciutto and a blood-orange vinaigrette, and you have a salad just right for an early spring first course. Serve with a chilled glass of crisp Sauvignon Blanc. If blood oranges are unavailable, substitute navel oranges.

Winter White Salad with a Hint of Green

1 SMALL HEAD ESCAROLE, TORN INTO 1$^1/_2$ (3.8CM) PIECES
2 BELGIAN ENDIVE, LEAVES SEPARATED
2 CELERY STALKS, CUT ON A SHARP DIAGONAL INTO THIN SLICES
1$^1/_2$ TABLESPOONS WHITE WINE VINEGAR
$^1/_4$ CUP (2 FL OZ/60ML) EXTRA-VIRGIN OLIVE OIL
SALT AND FRESHLY GROUND BLACK PEPPER
1 GRANNY SMITH OR PIPPIN APPLE, HALVED, CORED, AND THINLY SLICED
$^1/_2$ CUP (3$^1/_2$ OZ/75G) PECANS, TOASTED (SEE PAGE 78)
$^1/_3$ CUP (1$^1/_2$ OZ/45G) SHAVED PARMIGIANO REGGIANO CHEESE

In a bowl, toss together the escarole, endive, and celery.
Place in the refrigerator.

In a small bowl, whisk together the vinegar and olive oil.
Season to taste with salt and pepper.

To serve, toss the escarole, endive, and celery with the vinaigrette,
apples, pecans, and Parmigiano. Place in a salad bowl and
serve immediately.

SERVES 6

*S*o *reminiscent of the wine*
country is the aroma of a fire
made from vine trimmings in
the winter. That is a time I love
to head into the kitchen and cook.
And in the dead of winter, a crisp
salad is always welcome on the
table. This salad isn't completely
white; there's a hint of green on
the tips of the escarole and endive.
But I've always loved the creamy
white and ivories of winter.

Oven-Roasted Winter Vegetables

$1/_2$ POUND (225G) RUTABAGAS, PEELED AND CUT INTO 1-INCH
    (2.5-CM) PIECES
$1/_2$ POUND (225G) CARROTS, PEELED AND CUT INTO 1-INCH (2.5-CM) PIECES
$1/_2$ POUND (225G) PARSNIPS, PEELED AND CUT INTO 1-INCH
    (2.5-CM) PIECES
$1/_2$ POUND (225G) BRUSSELS SPROUTS, TRIMMED
$1/_2$ POUND (225G) SWEET POTATOES, CUT INTO 1-INCH (2.5-CM) PIECES
1 TABLESPOON UNSALTED BUTTER
1 TABLESPOON EXTRA-VIRGIN OLIVE OIL
2 TEASPOONS CHOPPED FRESH THYME
2 TEASPOONS CHOPPED FRESH SAGE
$1/_8$ TEASPOON FRESHLY GRATED NUTMEG
SALT AND FRESHLY GROUND BLACK PEPPER
$1/_2$ CUP (4 FL OZ/120ML) MARSALA

Preheat the oven to 450°F (230°C).

Bring a pot of salted water to a boil. Add the rutabagas, carrots, and parsnips and simmer until they give slightly when pierced with a fork, about 5 minutes.

Place the rutabagas, carrots, parsnips, Brussels sprouts, and sweet potatoes in a large roasting pan. Melt the butter in a small saucepan and stir in the oil, thyme, sage, and nutmeg. Drizzle the butter mixture over the vegetables and toss to coat them completely. Season to taste with salt and pepper. Pour the Marsala into the bottom of the roasting pan. Cover tightly with foil and bake in the oven for 40 minutes. Remove the foil, toss the vegetables, and continue to cook until the Marsala is evaporated and the vegetables can be easily pierced with a knife, 20 to 30 minutes.

Place the roasted vegetables on a platter and serve immediately.

SERVES 6

In the wine country, the soil is so rich and the climate so good that everyone has a garden year round. Winter doesn't necessarily have to mean that fresh vegetables are absent from the table. Instead offer winter root vegetables and tubers—rutabagas, carrots, parsnips—combined with sweet potatoes and Brussels sprouts. Serve with a roasted chicken or as a side dish with your Thanksgiving turkey.

Sugar Pumpkin Soup with Honey Pecan Butter

1 MEDIUM PUMPKIN, ABOUT 4 POUNDS (1.8KG)
3 TABLESPOONS (1 OZ/30G) TOASTED (SEE PAGE 78) AND FINELY CHOPPED
  PECANS
1 TABLESPOON HONEY
3 TABLESPOONS (1^1/$_2$ OZ/45G) BUTTER
2 SLICES BACON, DICED (ABOUT 2 OZ/60G)
1 LARGE YELLOW ONION, CHOPPED
6 CUPS (48 FL OZ/1.4L) CHICKEN STOCK
^{1}/$_2$ CUP (4 FL OZ/120ML) HEAVY CREAM
^{1}/$_4$ CUP (2 FL OZ/60ML) ORANGE JUICE
LARGE PINCH OF FRESHLY GRATED NUTMEG
SALT AND FRESHLY GROUND BLACK PEPPER
WHOLE LEAVES OF FLAT-LEAF PARSLEY AS A GARNISH

Preheat the oven to 375°F (190°C).

Halve the pumpkin from top to bottom and place it, cut side down, on an oiled baking sheet. Bake until the pumpkin can be easily skewered, 45 to 60 minutes. Cool for about 20 minutes. With a spoon, remove the seeds and discard. Scrape the pulp and reserve. Discard the skin.

For the honey-pecan butter, mash 2 tablespoons butter with the pecans and honey. Season to taste with salt and pepper. Roll the butter in plastic wrap into a cylindrical shape 1-inch (2.5cm) in diameter. Store in the refrigerator until well chilled and firm.

Melt the remaining 1 tablespoon of the butter in a soup pot over medium heat. Add the bacon and onions and cook, stirring occasionally, until the onions are soft and the bacon is just turning golden, about 7 minutes. Add the pumpkin and stock and simmer until the pumpkin falls apart, about 30 minutes. Let cool for about 20 minutes. In batches, puree the soup in a blender on high speed, 3 minutes per batch, until very smooth. Strain through a fine mesh strainer into a clean soup pot and add the cream, orange juice, and nutmeg. Season to taste with salt and pepper. If the soup is too thick, correct the consistency with additional water or stock.

Ladle the hot soup into soup bowls. Cut ^{1}/$_4$-inch (0.6cm) slices of the honey-pecan butter and float one in each bowl of soup. Garnish with parsley leaves and serve.

SERVES 6

I cherish my memories of autumn in New England. Just as the leaves start to turn, pumpkins and winter squash begin to show up at the farmer's market. I get nostalgic when I see the leaves on the grapevines turn from green to orange, crimson, and gold. At the same time, there is a chill in the air and I yearn for the flavors of my childhood.

Pumpkins and winter squash, with their thick skins, are quite durable. When stored in the coolest place in the house, they will last for months. If pumpkin is unavailable, substitute butternut or turban squash.

Artichokes Stewed with Olive Oil, Lemon, and Plenty of Garlic

5 LEMONS

36 SMALL ARTICHOKES OR 12 MEDIUM ARTICHOKES

10 SPRIGS OF THYME

5 BAY LEAVES

20 GARLIC CLOVES, PEELED AND HALVED

3/4 CUP (6 FL OZ/180ML) EXTRA-VIRGIN OLIVE OIL

1 TEASPOON SALT

With a vegetable peeler, remove the zest from the lemons.

Prepare a large bowl of water to which you have added the juice of 1 lemon. Remove the tough outer leaves of the artichokes. Working with 1 artichoke at a time, cut off the top half of the artichokes, including all of the prickly leaf points. Remove the tough outer leaves of the artichoke until you get to the very light green leaves. Pare the stem to reveal the light green center. If you are using large artichokes, cut each one in half lengthwise, then scoop out the prickly chokes and discard. Cut in half again. As each is cut, place in the bowl of lemon water.

Drain the artichokes and place them in a saucepan with the juice of the remaining 4 lemons, the lemon peel, thyme, bay leaves, garlic, olive oil, and salt. Add water just to cover. Cover the pan with a piece of parchment and weight the parchment with a small plate that fits inside the pan. Over medium-high heat, bring to a boil, turn down to medium, and simmer for 5 minutes. Turn off and let the pan cool completely, about 1 hour.

Divide the mixture between 2 quart (liter) jars and store in the refrigerator until ready to use. They keep for 2 weeks in the refrigerator.

MAKES 2 QUARTS (LITERS)

Castroville, California, a couple of hours south of the wine country, is considered the artichoke capital of the United States. In the early spring, these thorny blossoms called artichokes shoot from silver-green leaves that resemble saw blades. If it's a good year, the artichoke farmer harvests another smaller crop in the autumn. When he has a surplus, here's one solution.

Garlic

IN THE MEDITERRANEAN, garlic is used generously in every country, its flavor dominating the kitchen. It's the same in California, where the town of Gilroy boasts that it is the "garlic capital of the world."

In the early spring, garlic sprouts from the ground, resembling a bulbous green onion. Later in the spring, the immature garlic, called green garlic, can be pulled from the ground. Green garlic is not nearly as assertive as mature garlic, and is perfect for soups, savory flans, and soufflés, in which the flavor of garlic is meant to perfume—not overpower—the dish. During the summer months, mature bulbs of garlic, stronger in flavor, are ready to be pulled from the ground. They can be used immediately or dried hung in a cool, dark place for use during the fall and winter months.

But garlic goes beyond the function of just flavoring food. Today, it's hard to avoid hearing about the positive effects of the Mediterranean diet, rich with vegetables, grains, olive oil, and plenty of garlic.

So grill a slice or two of great bread and rub garlic over it, using the rough texture of the bread as a grater. Drizzle with fruity virgin olive oil and add a sprinkling of coarse salt. Now that's good eating!

Artichoke Fritters
with Meyer Lemon Mayonnaise

1 CUP PLUS 2 TABLESPOONS (5 OZ/130G) ALL-PURPOSE FLOUR

SALT

2 TEASPOONS GRATED LEMON ZEST

2 EGGS, SEPARATED

3 TABLESPOONS OLIVE OIL

JUICE OF 1 LEMON

3/4 CUP (6 FL OZ/180ML) WARM BEER

6 LARGE ARTICHOKES

FRESHLY GROUND BLACK PEPPER

CORN OR PEANUT OIL, FOR DEEP FRYING

MEYER LEMON MAYONNAISE (SEE NEXT PAGE)

WHOLE FLAT-LEAF PARSLEY LEAVES AS A GARNISH

Sift the flour, 1/2 teaspoon salt, and lemon zest together in a bowl. Make a well in the center and add the beaten egg yolks, 1 tablespoon olive oil, 1 tablespoon lemon juice, and the beer. Mix well with a whisk. Let the mixture rest for 1 hour at room temperature.

In the meantime, have ready a large bowl of water to which you have added the remaining lemon juice. Cut off the top half of the artichokes, including all of the prickly leaf points. Remove the tough outer leaves of the artichoke until you get to the very light green leaves. Pare the stem to reveal the light green center. Cut each artichoke in half lengthwise, then scoop out the prickly chokes and discard. Cut the artichokes into thin wedges lengthwise. Place each wedge in the bowl with lemon water as it is cut.

Warm the remaining 2 tablespoons olive oil over medium heat in a skillet. Drain the artichokes and add to the pan with 1/2 cup water and a large pinch of salt and pepper. Cover and cook until the liquid evaporates, about 15 minutes. Let cool.

In a deep saucepan, add oil to a depth of 2 inches. Heat to 375°F (190°C) when tested with a thermometer or until a drop of the batter sizzles on contact. Meanwhile, in a bowl, beat the egg whites until stiff. Gently fold the egg whites and artichokes into the batter.

Drop the mixture by heaping tablespoons into the hot oil; do not overcrowd the pan. Fry, turning often, until golden brown, about 2 minutes. Using a slotted spoon, transfer to paper towels to drain.

To serve, arrange the hot fritters on a platter. Garnish with Meyer Lemon Mayonnaise and parsley.

SERVES 6

*W*hen you eat an artichoke, you're actually eating a flower bud. If the bud were allowed to flower, it would reveal a large, violet-blue blossom. But artichokes hardly ever get that far—instead they are eaten and enjoyed at the bud stage.

Meyer Lemon Mayonnaise

1 EGG YOLK
1 TEASPOON DIJON MUSTARD
1/2 CUP (4 FL OZ/120 ML) PURE OLIVE OIL
1/2 CUP (4 FL OZ/120 ML) PEANUT, VEGETABLE, CORN, OR SAFFLOWER OIL
2 CLOVES GARLIC, MINCED OR MASHED WITH A MORTAR AND PESTLE
JUICE OF 1 MEYER LEMON
SALT AND FRESHLY GROUND BLACK PEPPER

In a small bowl, whisk the yolk, mustard, and 1 tablespoon olive oil together until an emulsion is formed. Combine the olive oil and the peanut oil. Drop by drop, add the oil to the emulsion, whisking constantly. Continue to do this, drop by drop, in a steady stream, whisking until all of the oil has been added. Do not add the oil too quickly and be sure that the emulsion is homogeneous before adding more oil. Season with garlic, lemon, and salt and pepper.

Add 2 or 3 tablespoons warm water to the mayonnaise, whisking constantly, to thin the mayonnaise to make a fluid sauce. This mayonnaise should be used the day it is made.

MAKES ABOUT 1 CUP

*M*eyer lemons, probably a cross between a lemon and an orange, make a particularly mellow mayonnaise.

Salad of Frisée, Radicchio, Pears, Pomegranates, and Persimmons

1/2 CUP (4 FL OZ/120 ML) DRY RIESLING OR GEWÜRZTRAMINER
1 TABLESPOON SHERRY VINEGAR
3 TABLESPOONS (1 1/2 FL OZ/45 ML) EXTRA-VIRGIN OLIVE OIL
SALT AND FRESHLY GROUND BLACK PEPPER
2 LARGE BUNCHES FRISÉE, ENDS TRIMMED
1 SMALL HEAD RADICCHIO, TORN INTO 2-INCH (5-CM) PIECES
1 FUYU PERSIMMON, CUT INTO THIN SLICES
1 RED BARTLETT PEAR, HALVED, CORED, AND CUT INTO THIN SLICES
6 FIGS, HALVED
1 SMALL POMEGRANATE, PEELED, SEEDS REMOVED AND SEPARATED
1/2 CUP (2 1/2 OZ/75G) WALNUT HALVES, TOASTED (SEE PAGE 78)

*S*o often people think they can't serve wine with a salad because the acidity of the vinaigrette isn't wine-friendly. I've discovered a great way to combat this problem. Reduce some wine until it is nearly a syrup and use it in place of a good portion of the vinegar. Serve the same kind of wine you reduced. This is the answer to your wine/salad problem.

In a small saucepan over high heat, reduce the wine until 1 to 2 tablespoons remain. Let cool. In a small bowl, whisk together the vinegar, reduced wine, and olive oil and season to taste with salt and pepper.

Place the frisée, radicchio, persimmon slices, pear slices, and figs in a bowl. Add the vinaigrette and gently toss together. Place on individual salad plates. Garnish with pomegranate seeds and walnut halves and serve immediately.

Serves 6

Salad of Greens, Shaved Mushrooms, Asparagus, and Truffle Oil

12 MEDIUM CHANTERELLES (ABOUT 3 OZ/90G)
12 STALKS OF TENDER ASPARAGUS, ENDS TRIMMED (ABOUT 4 OZ/120G)
2 TABLESPOONS WHITE TRUFFLE OIL
$1/4$ CUP (2 FL OZ/60ML) EXTRA-VIRGIN OLIVE OIL
$2^1/_2$ TABLESPOONS ($1^1/_4$ FL OZ/40ML) CHAMPAGNE VINEGAR
1 SMALL SHALLOT, MINCED
SALT AND FRESHLY GROUND BLACK PEPPER
8 CUPS (16 OZ/480G) FRESH MIXED BABY SALAD GREENS

With a cheese shaver or mandoline, shave the mushrooms into paper-thin slices. With a knife, cut the asparagus on a diagonal into paper-thin slices.

In a bowl, whisk together the truffle oil, olive oil, champagne vinegar, and shallots. Season to taste with salt and pepper.

To serve, place the salad greens, mushrooms, and asparagus in a large bowl. Add the vinaigrette and toss together. Place on serving plates, mounding the salad in the middle of each plate. Serve immediately.

Serves 6

I would love to take credit for this salad but it was inspired from my years cooking at Chez Panisse, where fresh vegetables and bright flavors are of paramount importance. Try this technique of shaving thin slivers of fresh mushrooms and combining them with asparagus, crisp salad greens, and a truffle vinaigrette. If fresh, unblemished chanterelles are unavailable, substitute button or other cultivated mushrooms.

Fava Bean, Fennel, and Parsley Salad

Once when I was teaching in Napa, I wanted to make this fava bean and farfalle pasta salad for a crowd. To do so, we needed to shell about ten pounds of favas. I gathered several of the students around a big table, gave them each a glass of wine, and in no time they were done. Shelling the beans was a bit of an effort, but they told me the results were well worth the trouble.

4 POUNDS (3.6KG) FRESH FAVA BEANS IN THE PODS
2 MEDIUM FRESH FENNEL BULBS, TRIMMED
1/4 CUP (2 FL OZ/60ML) EXTRA-VIRGIN OLIVE OIL
2 TABLESPOONS LEMON JUICE
1 GARLIC CLOVE, MINCED
SALT AND FRESHLY GROUND BLACK PEPPER
2 LARGE BUNCHES FRESH FLAT-LEAF PARSLEY,
    LEAVES PICKED AND STEMS DISCARDED

Remove the fava beans from their pods and discard the pods. Bring a pot of water to a boil, add the fava beans, and boil 30 seconds. Drain, cool, and shell the beans. Season with salt and pepper and reserve.

With a sharp knife, a mandoline, or an electric meat slicer, shave the fennel into paper-thin slices and reserve.

In a small bowl, whisk together the olive oil, lemon juice, and garlic. Season to taste with salt and pepper.

In a bowl, toss together the fava beans, fennel, parsley, and vinaigrette. Place on a platter and serve immediately.

SERVES 6

Worth the Trouble

PEOPLE ARE SO AFRAID of fava beans, but once you know how easy they are to work with, you too will buy a big bag of them when you see the first of the season.

Fava beans come to us in the spring. I remember picking the first fava beans of the season in Italy. They were so tiny, like candy that you could pop them in your mouth.

Fava beans are those large pods you see in the market, whether they are brilliant green at the beginning of the season or bruised with black a little later on.

First of all, you need to peel them. The easiest way to do this is to snap the pods where you feel a fava bean and pop the bean out of the pod. If the beans are tender and young, about the size of a large pea, you can use them just like this or blanch them in boiling water for 10 seconds. The Italians love to celebrate the fava harvest by drizzling the fresh raw beans with fruity virgin olive oil, sprinkling them with sea salt, and shaving a bit of Parmigiano Reggiano over the top.

When they get a bit older, the fava's flavor is more pronounced. The size of the bean ranges from a flattened-out marble to a boulder. It is best, after peeling them, to bring a pot of water to a boil. Add the fava beans and blanch them for 20 to 25 seconds. Immediately remove them with a slotted spoon. When the beans have cooled enough to handle, make a small slit with your fingernail in the side of the skin and pop the bright green bean out of the skin. Discard the skins.

Yes, fava beans are a bit of work, but they are definitely worth the trouble.

Spinach and Ricotta Gnocchi
with Wilted Greens

2 POUNDS (1.8KG) SPINACH, STEMS REMOVED, WASHED, DRIED,
  AND CHOPPED

1$\frac{1}{4}$ CUPS (5 OZ/150G) GRATED PARMIGIANO REGGIANO CHEESE

1$\frac{1}{2}$ TO 2 CUPS (6 TO 8 OZ/180 TO 240G) ALL-PURPOSE FLOUR

1 CUP (8 OZ/240G) WHOLE-MILK RICOTTA CHEESE, DRAINED
  FOR 2 HOURS IN A CHEESECLOTH-LINED SIEVE

2 EGGS

$\frac{1}{2}$ TEASPOON FRESHLY GRATED NUTMEG

SALT AND FRESHLY GROUND BLACK PEPPER

1 CUP (8 FL OZ/240ML) CHICKEN STOCK

2 TABLESPOONS EXTRA-VIRGIN OLIVE OIL

2 BUNCHES GREENS, SUCH AS SWISS CHARD, TURNIP GREENS, ESCAROLE,
  OR BEET GREENS, CUT INTO 1-INCH (2.5CM) STRIPS

1 TEASPOON GRATED LEMON ZEST

1 GARLIC CLOVE, MINCED

PINCH OF CRUSHED RED PEPPER FLAKES

1 TABLESPOON LEMON JUICE

"*I* thought gnocchi were those heavy dumplings made with potatoes!" one of my students said with a frown. I am sure she was remembering poorly made doughy balls that fell to the pit of her stomach with a thud. I reminded her there are all sorts of gnocchi. They can be heavy if they are made incorrectly, and they can also be as light as a cloud, as evidenced here with these gnocchi that melt in your mouth.

Place the spinach in a large skillet over medium heat. Cook, tossing it constantly, until wilted, about 2 minutes. Remove the spinach from the pan and wring out excess moisture in a clean kitchen towel. Chop and place the spinach in a bowl with $\frac{1}{2}$ cup grated Parmigiano, $\frac{1}{2}$ cup (2 oz/60g) of the flour, the ricotta, eggs, nutmeg, and salt and pepper and mix well. Add additional flour until the mixture is no longer sticky.

Bring a large pot of salted water to a boil. With a spoon, shape the dough into large, oval, walnut-size balls and roll them in the remaining 1 cup (4 oz/120g) flour. Place the gnocchi in the water, a few at a time, and after they rise to the surface, continue to simmer until firm to the touch, 5 to 10 minutes. Remove with a slotted spoon and place in a well-oiled 2-quart (2-liter) baking dish. Roll the gnocchi to coat them with oil.

Preheat the oven to 400°F (200°C).

Pour the chicken stock into a small saucepan. Boil rapidly until reduced to $\frac{1}{2}$ cup (4 fl oz/120ml). Set aside.

Heat the olive oil in a large skillet over high heat until hot. Add the greens and toss until the greens wilt, 3 to 4 minutes. Add the lemon zest, garlic, and crushed red pepper. Add the reduced chicken stock and lemon juice and toss until hot, about 30 seconds. Season to taste with salt and pepper.

Ten minutes before serving, place the gnocchi in the oven for 10 minutes, or until warm. To serve, place the gnocchi on a serving platter and top with the greens. Sprinkle the top with $^1/_4$ cup (1 oz/30g) of the Parmigiano. Pass the remaining $^1/_2$ cup (2 oz/60g) Parmigiano at the table.

MAKES 36 DUMPLINGS AND SERVES 6

Fusilli with Summer Beans and Savory

$2^1/_2$ POUNDS (1.1KG) ASSORTED FRESH SHELL BEANS, CRANBERRY,
    LIMA, SCARLET RUNNER, BLACK-EYED PEAS, ABOUT 1 CUP
    ($6^1/_2$ OZ/200G) SHELLED
$1^1/_4$ POUND (500G) ASSORTMENT OF STRING BEANS, GREEN, YELLOW,
    OR HARICOT VERT, TRIMMED
SALT
$2^1/_2$ CUPS (20 FL OZ/600ML) CHICKEN STOCK
2 TABLESPOONS EXTRA-VIRGIN OLIVE OIL
2 SHALLOTS, MINCED
2 GARLIC CLOVES, MINCED
2 TABLESPOONS CHOPPED FRESH FLAT-LEAF PARSLEY
2 TABLESPOON CHOPPED FRESH SUMMER SAVORY
2 TEASPOONS CHOPPED FRESH OREGANO
FRESHLY GROUND BLACK PEPPER
10 OUNCES (300G) FUSILLI
SUMMER SAVORY SPRIGS AS A GARNISH

Fresh summer beans seem to ripen in the garden all at the same time. Here I've combined fresh-from-the-garden shell beans with green or yellow string beans, pasta, and summer savory, for a celebration of the bounty of summer.

Shell the beans. In a large pot of boiling water over high heat, cook the shelled beans until tender, 5 to 10 minutes. Drain and cool. Cut the string beans in half crosswise on the diagonal. In a large pot of boiling salted water over high heat, cook the string beans until tender, 4 to 6 minutes. Drain and cool.

Bring the stock to a boil and reduce by half. Remove from the heat.

In a large frying pan over medium heat, heat the olive oil and cook the shallots until soft, 5 minutes. Add the garlic and stir 1 minute. Add the shell beans, string beans, parsley, savory, oregano, and reduced stock. Stir together until warm, about 1 minute. Season with salt and pepper.

Bring a large pot of salted water to a boil. Add the pasta and cook until the pasta is al dente, 8 to 10 minutes. Drain and toss with the bean mixture. Place in a bowl and serve, garnished with savory sprigs.

SERVES 6

Crispy Polenta Cakes
with Wild Mushroom Ragout

SALT

1 CUP (5 OZ/150G) COARSE POLENTA

1/2 CUP (2 OZ/60G) GRATED PARMIGIANO REGGIANO CHEESE

4 TABLESPOONS (2 OZ/60G) UNSALTED BUTTER, AT ROOM TEMPERATURE

FRESHLY GROUND BLACK PEPPER

2 TABLESPOONS CHOPPED FRESH FLAT-LEAF PARSLEY

2 GARLIC CLOVES, MINCED

2 TEASPOONS EXTRA-VIRGIN OLIVE OIL

1 POUND (450G) MIXED FRESH WILD MUSHROOMS, TRIMMED AND SLICED

3 CUPS (24 FL OZ/725ML) CHICKEN STOCK

1/2 CUP (4 FL OZ/120ML) HEAVY CREAM

2 CUPS (8 OZ/225G) ALL-PURPOSE FLOUR FOR DUSTING THE POLENTA

1 CUP (8 FL OZ/240ML) OLIVE OIL FOR FRYING

After the grape harvest, when there is a chill in the air, we are always looking for hearty dishes in the wine country. I always turn to wild mushrooms. But don't buy wild mushrooms after a heavy rain. If you do, you're spending money on rain water. Instead, buy them when they're dry and unblemished. Clean them by brushing lightly; never immerse them in water.

Bring 6 cups (48 fl oz/1.4 L) of water and 1 teaspoon salt to a boil. Lower the heat to medium and slowly add the cornmeal in a shower, whisking constantly until the mixture thickens, 3 to 5 minutes. Change to a wooden spoon and continue to simmer, stirring occasionally, until the spoon stands in the polenta, 15 to 25 minutes. Add the Parmigiano and 2 tablespoons of the butter and mix well. Season with salt and pepper. Immediately spread the polenta in a buttered 9- x 9-inch (23 x 23-cm) pan. Smooth the top with a rubber spatula and refrigerate. Combine the parsley and garlic and chop together until very fine. Reserve.

In a large skillet, melt the remaining 2 tablespoons butter with the extra-virgin olive oil over high heat. Add the button and wild mushrooms and cook, stirring occasionally, until golden and the mushroom liquid has evaporated, 7 to 10 minutes. Remove the mushrooms and set aside. Add the chicken stock, cream, garlic, and parsley to the pan and simmer to reduce by half, 6 to 8 minutes. Season with salt and pepper.

Score the polenta into six 3 x 4^1/$_2$-inch (7.5 x 12-cm) squares. Halve each square diagonally to make 2 triangles. Remove from the pan and toss the polenta triangles carefully in flour to dust them lightly.

Heat ^{1}/$_2$ inch (1.25 cm) of olive oil in a large, deep frying pan until the oil sizzles and a tiny piece of polenta turns golden on contact, 375°F (190°C). Add a few of the polenta triangles and cook, turning occasionally, until golden on both sides. Drain on paper towels.

To serve, place 2 hot polenta triangles on each plate. Warm the mushroom ragout and spoon over the polenta. Serve immediately.

SERVES 6

Fettuccine with Tomatoes, Basil, and Crisp Bread Crumbs

1 CUP VERY COARSE FRESH BREAD CRUMBS

6 TABLESPOONS (3 FL OZ/90ML) EXTRA-VIRGIN OLIVE OIL

SALT AND FRESHLY GROUND BLACK PEPPER

$3^1/_2$ TABLESPOONS ($1^3/_4$ FL OZ/50ML) BALSAMIC VINEGAR

2 CUPS (10 OZ/300G) YELLOW CHERRY TOMATOES, HALVED

2 CUPS (10 OZ/300G) RED CHERRY TOMATOES, HALVED

12 OUNCES (350G) FETTUCCINE

$^1/_2$ CUP (1 OZ/30G) BASIL LEAVES, CUT INTO THIN STRIPS

Preheat the oven to 375°F (190°C).

Place the bread crumbs on a baking sheet. Drizzle with 2 tablespoons of the olive oil and toss the crumbs to distribute the oil evenly. Season the bread crumbs with salt and pepper. Bake in the middle of the oven, tossing occasionally, until they turn golden brown, 8 to 10 minutes. Remove from the oven and let cool.

In a bowl, whisk together the remaining 4 tablespoons (2 fl oz/60ml) olive oil and the balsamic vinegar. Season to taste with salt and pepper. Add the tomatoes and stir together. Set aside.

Fill a large pot three-fourths full of salted water and bring to a boil. Add the pasta and cook until al dente, 10 to 12 minutes or according to the directions on the package.

Drain the pasta and toss with the tomatoes and vinaigrette. Place in a serving bowl and garnish with basil and bread crumbs. Serve immediately.

SERVES 6

I don't think there's any better combination than tomatoes and basil. Pick vine-ripened tomatoes at their height of sweetness and combine them with tender leaves of young basil. This is what summer should be—and every season for that matter, when the best peak-of-season ingredients stand by themselves and make the finished dish shine.

Farmer's Market Risotto
with Zucchini and Their Blossoms

1 POUND (450G) BABY ZUCCHINI, BLOSSOMS ATTACHED
3 CUPS (24 FL OZ/1.4L) CHICKEN STOCK
2 TABLESPOONS EXTRA-VIRGIN OLIVE OIL
1 SMALL YELLOW ONION, MINCED
1$\frac{1}{2}$ CUPS (8 OZ/225G) ARBORIO, VIALONE NANO, OR CARNAROLI RICE
$\frac{1}{2}$ CUP (4 FL OZ/120ML) DRY WHITE WINE, SUCH AS SAUVIGNON BLANC
SALT
2 TABLESPOONS CHOPPED FRESH FLAT-LEAF PARSLEY
2 TABLESPOONS UNSALTED BUTTER, AT ROOM TEMPERATURE
1 CUP (4 OZ/120G) FINELY GRATED PARMIGIANO REGGIANO CHEESE
FRESHLY GROUND BLACK PEPPER

When you visit your farmer's market at the crest of summer and find tender young zucchini with their bright yellow flowers still attached, grab a basket. They're great for stuffing, frying, and most of all, for zucchini risotto. Stir the blossoms into the almost-finished dish for a splash of color and a bit of peppery flavor.

Remove the flowers from the zucchini and slice the zucchini into $\frac{1}{4}$-inch (0.6cm) slices. Cut the blossoms into thirds crosswise.

In a saucepan, combine the chicken stock and 3 cups (24 fl oz/1.4L) of water and bring to a boil over high heat. Reduce the heat to low and maintain just below the boiling point on a back burner of the stove.

Heat the olive oil in a large, heavy frying pan over medium heat. Add the onions and cook until soft, about 7 minutes. Add the zucchini and cook for 1 minute. Add the rice and stir to coat the rice with oil until the edges of the rice are translucent and there is a white dot in the center of each grain, about 3 minutes. Add the wine and cook, stirring, until the wine evaporates, about 1 minute. Add 1/4 teaspoon of salt and about 1 cup (8 fl oz/240ml) of the stock and stir the rice constantly to wipe it away from the bottom and sides of the pot. When most of the liquid has been absorbed but the rice is still loose, add another ladleful of stock and continue to cook the risotto. Continue to add stock a ladle at a time, stirring constantly, until the rice is just beyond the chalky stage, 18 to 22 minutes. If you run out of stock, add hot water.

Remove from the stove and stir in the another ladleful of stock, the parsley, butter, zucchini blossoms, and half the Parmigiano. Season to taste with salt and pepper. Cover and let sit off the heat for 5 minutes.

To serve, remove the cover, stir, and serve immediately, sprinkled with the remaining Parmigiano.

SERVES 6

Just hearing the words "farmstead cheese" makes me feel happy. There's something thrilling— and deeply reassuring—about a cheese made right on the farm where the milk was produced. I think of rich, creamy goat cheese; tangy, aged pecorino; silky-smooth crescenza—cheeses made by hand in small batches by individuals who take pride in what they do. And I think of my grandmother, who made fabulous cheeses with fresh milk from the cows on her dairy farm.

Her farmer's cheese, the simplest of all to make, was my favorite. She'd start by setting some of the milk from the afternoon milking on the back burner of her stove—with no heat under it, mind you, just the residual warmth from the day's cooking and baking. Over the next couple of days, like a small miracle, the milk would sour and curdle, forming curds and whey.

Then she'd throw in a bit of salt and ladle the curds into a cheesecloth pouch about the size of a lunch bag. She'd tie a fat knot at one end of the pouch and hang it on a special nail over the sink, and for hours, the kitchen would be filled with a familiar ping. . . ping. . . ping. . ., as the whey dripped slowly away, leaving just the curds.

By the next morning the pouch was half its original size and looked like a deflated balloon. My grandmother would lay it on the drain board of the sink and cover it with a smooth, old piece of barn wood weighted down with a large, flat rock. Over the next few days, the cheese would take form and lose most of its moisture. And on the fifth day, with the excitement of a kid under a Christmas tree, I'd help my grandmother peel away the cheesecloth, revealing the fresh, soft cheese, all creamy and white and glistening. I'll never forget the fun of slicing off big slabs of that cheese and eating them on crusty rye bread.

Today, a new crop of small farmers and cheese makers—many based right here in Northern California—are discovering the beauty of farmstead and artisanal cheeses. As a life-long cheese lover, I'm delighted. And, as I researched this book, I was even more

Cheeses

CHEESES

A herd of Holstein cattle in Northern California.
Opposite: Young goats at Redwood Hill Farm, Sebastopol, California.

delighted to have the chance to visit some of them.

One morning not long ago, I headed up to Sebastopol to Redwood Hill Farm, where Steven Schack and Jennifer Lynn produce wonderful goat cheeses. Their directions were sketchy and

A selection of cheeses from Tomales Bay Foods in Point Reyes Station, California.

the road was winding, but when I was about to give up hope, the farm appeared, just as they had described it, tucked away in a grove of redwoods at a bend in the road.

Before entering the creamery, I was told I'd have to dress the part. I put on a white lab coat and pulled on a mesh hair net and a pair of high rubber boots. As I stepped into the sudsy bath to rinse off my boots, I thought I must be quite a sight.

We made cheese all day, cutting the curds, putting the fresh cheese into molds, turning the dried cheeses, and rotating the cheeses in the aging room. As I worked with Steven and Jennifer, I learned that they use traditional European cheese-making practices and frequently visit small farms in France to study their craft.

Later, they even let me try my hand at milking a goat—with mixed success. Somehow, it had seemed easier when I was a kid at my grandparents' farm!

Another day, I traveled across the hills to Valley Ford, near Petaluma, to visit Cindy Callahan at Bellweather Farms. I'd known Cindy from my days at Chez Panisse, where we used to cook the lamb she raised. Now, her interests have shifted to breeding dairy sheep for cheese making, and she produces some of the finest sheep's milk cheeses in America.

As Cindy and I trudged up the hill to a rough wooden barn surrounded by sheep and lambs, we chatted about old times and about her new life in the world of cheese. Like Steven and Jennifer at Redwood Hill, the Callahans use traditional methods practiced by small cheese makers all over the world, their main inspiration being the cheeses of Italy. Everything is done by hand. For the next several hours, I watched Cindy and her son make pecorino, a hard, Italian-style sheep's milk cheese.

As the sun was setting, we made our way back down the hill to the house below. I glanced back over my shoulder, and there—standing peacefully on the slope—were all the little lambs and sheep, looking contentedly at us. I smiled and thought about the spirit of the honest, passionate commitment you feel when you visit farms like these. These people are not just making great cheese. They are making art out of the simple bounty of nature.

Brown Butter, Walnut, and Cheddar Wafers

6 TABLESPOONS (3 OZ/90G) UNSALTED BUTTER
1 CUP (4 OZ/120G) GRATED EXTRA-SHARP CHEDDAR CHEESE
1 TABLESPOON DRY MUSTARD
$1/4$ TEASPOON CAYENNE
SALT
1 CUP (4 OZ/120G) ALL-PURPOSE FLOUR
1 TEASPOON BAKING POWDER
1 EGG
$1/4$ CUP (1 OZ/30G) WALNUTS, TOASTED (SEE PAGE 78) AND FINELY GROUND

Place the butter in a saucepan over medium-high heat. Cook until the butter melts and the tiny solids on the bottom turn brown and begin to smoke slightly, 2 to 3 minutes. Immediately remove from the heat.

Place the butter, cheese, mustard, cayenne, $1/2$ teaspoon salt, the flour, and baking powder in the bowl of the food processor. Process until well mixed, 1 to 2 minutes. Place in a bowl, cover with plastic wrap, and chill in the refrigerator for 1 hour.

Divide the dough into 2 pieces and form each piece into a 1-inch (2.5-cm) cylinder. Wrap tightly in plastic wrap and roll to smooth the edges. Chill in the freezer for 20 minutes.

Preheat the oven to 350°F (175°C).

For the glaze, whisk the egg with 1 teaspoon water.

Remove the plastic from the dough and cut into $1/4$-inch (0.6cm) discs. Sprinkle a baking sheet with 2 tablespoons water. Place the crackers on the baking sheet 1 inch (2.5cm) apart. Brush with the glaze and sprinkle with toasted walnuts. Bake until golden, about 15 minutes. Remove from the pan and let cool.

Serve hot or room temperature.

MAKES ABOUT 4 TO 5 DOZEN CRACKERS

A few years ago, homemade crackers were featured in every magazine. When you had drinks at a friend's house, there they were, gussied up with hot pepper and sharp cheese. Still, despite the overexposure, there is nothing like them. Make the cracker dough ahead of time and store it in the freezer. When you need crackers, slice and bake. Or bake them and store them in an airtight container for up to a week.

Asparagus Cheese Puffs

8 OUNCES (240G) ASPARAGUS, ENDS TRIMMED
$^3/_4$ CUP (6 FL OZ/185ML) WHOLE MILK
5 TABLESPOONS (2$^1/_2$ OZ/75G) UNSALTED BUTTER, CUT INTO 10 PIECES
$^1/_2$ TEASPOON SALT
$^3/_4$ CUP (3 OZ/90G) ALL-PURPOSE FLOUR
$^1/_4$ TEASPOON CAYENNE
3 EGGS, AT ROOM TEMPERATURE
1 CUP (3 OZ/90G) COARSELY GRATED DRY SHEEP'S MILK CHEESE,
    SUCH AS PECORINO OR MANCHEGO
$^1/_2$ CUP (2 OZ/60G) FINELY GRATED PARMIGIANO REGGIANO CHEESE

I discovered the cheese course when I went to France for the first time. I still remember a cart being wheeled to my table with 20 to 30 different types of cheese. Now that's my idea of heaven! This recipe uses any sheep's milk cheese, Parmigiano, lots of fresh asparagus, and a dash of cayenne.

Cut the asparagus into $^1/_4$-inch (0.6cm) lengths. Bring a medium saucepan of salted water to a boil. Add the asparagus and simmer until just tender, about 1 minute. Strain immediately and reserve.

In a heavy saucepan, bring the milk and butter to a boil. In the meantime, sift together the salt, flour, and cayenne. As soon as the milk comes to a boil and the butter has melted, remove the pan from the heat and add the flour mixture all at once. With a wooden spoon, beat the mixture until it thickens and pulls away from the sides of the pan, about 1 minute. Transfer the mixture to a bowl. Add the eggs, one at a time, beating well after each addition. Do not add another egg until the previous one has been thoroughly incorporated. Let cool 10 minutes.

Preheat the oven to 400°F (200°C). Line 2 baking sheets with lightly buttered baking parchment.

Add the asparagus, sheep's milk cheese, and Parmigiano to the dough and mix together. Spoon rounded teaspoons of the dough onto the baking sheets 1 inch apart. Bake in the middle of the oven until golden brown, 20 to 25 minutes. Remove the puffs from the parchment and serve immediately.

MAKES 36 PUFFS AND SERVES 6

Crostini with Feta and Hot Red Pepper

1¼ CUPS (10 FL OZ/300ML) YOGURT, DRAINED IN A PAPER-TOWEL LINED
    SIEVE FOR 4 HOURS

SALT

10 OUNCES (300G) FETA CHEESE

2 GARLIC CLOVES, MINCED

½ TO ¾ TEASPOON CAYENNE

1 TEASPOON SWEET PAPRIKA

1 TABLESPOON PLUS 1 TEASPOON EXTRA-VIRGIN OLIVE OIL

IMPORTED BLACK OLIVES AS A GARNISH

12 SLICES COARSE-TEXTURED COUNTRY-STYLE BREAD, TOASTED AND CUT
    INTO 2-INCH (5-CM) PIECES

Place the yogurt, ¼ teaspoon salt, and the feta in a bowl and mash together with a fork to make a smooth paste. Add the garlic, cayenne, paprika, and 1 tablespoon olive oil and mix well. Alternately, this can be pureed in the food processor or blender.

Spread the puree on a serving plate. Drizzle with the remaining 1 teaspoon olive oil and garnish with olives. Serve with toasted bread.

SERVES 6

This dish was inspired by a trip to Turkey years ago. I was in the mountains, surrounded by sheep and wooden barrels filled with feta in brine. The cheese maker gave me his favorite recipe using feta. "Simple!" he said. Now some delicious feta cheese is being made in California. Try it in this recipe!

Wild Mushroom and Blue Cheese Crostini

*ou really have to know what
you're doing to forage for wild
mushrooms. I can remember
my grandmother bringing back
big baskets from the woods.
My mother would look at them
with a discerning eye. Those in
the know are in for a treat when
wild mushrooms pop up everywhere during the fall and again
after the spring rains. The rest of
us can buy delicious mushrooms
at most well-stocked markets
during the autumn months
and again in the spring.*

2 TABLESPOONS EXTRA-VIRGIN OLIVE OIL
$^1/_2$ POUND (225G) WILD MUSHROOMS, THINLY SLICED
$^1/_2$ POUND (225G) CULTIVATED MUSHROOMS, THINLY SLICED
1 TABLESPOON CHOPPED FRESH FLAT-LEAF PARSLEY
1 TEASPOON CHOPPED FRESH THYME
1 TEASPOON CHOPPED FRESH MINT
SALT AND FRESHLY GROUND BLACK PEPPER
1 CUP (4 OZ/120G) COARSELY GRATED FONTINA CHEESE
$^1/_2$ CUP (2 OZ/60G) CRUMBLED GORGONZOLA CHEESE
2 GARLIC CLOVES, PEELED
12 SLICES COARSE-TEXTURED COUNTRY-STYLE BREAD, TOASTED
2 TABLESPOONS LEMON JUICE
WHOLE LEAVES OF FLAT-LEAF PARSLEY AS A GARNISH

In a large skillet over medium-high heat, heat the olive oil. Add the
mushrooms and cook, stirring occasionally, until golden and the liquid
has evaporated, 7 to 10 minutes. Add the parsley, thyme, and mint, and
toss together. Season well with salt and pepper. Remove from the heat.
Let cool and add the cheese. Toss together.

Preheat the broiler.

Rub each side of the toast lightly with garlic. Distribute the mushrooms
and cheese on top of the toast. Place the toasts on a baking sheet in
a single layer and broil until the cheese melts, about 1 minute. Transfer
to a platter and drizzle with lemon juice. Serve immediately, garnished
with parsley leaves.

SERVES 6

Toasted Goat Cheese Salad with Smoked Bacon

3 SMALL ROUNDS FRESH GOAT CHEESE, ABOUT 5 OUNCES (150G) EACH

$1/2$ CUP (4 FL OZ/120ML) EXTRA-VIRGIN OLIVE OIL

8 SPRIGS OF FRESH THYME

8 SPRIGS OF FRESH OREGANO

2 SPRIGS OF FRESH ROSEMARY

4 OUNCES (120G) SMOKED BACON, CUT INTO $1/2$-INCH (1.25-CM) DICE

4 THICK SLICES COARSE-TEXTURED COUNTRY-STYLE BREAD, TORN INTO
$1/2$-INCH (1.25-CM) CUBES

$1/2$ TEASPOON DIJON MUSTARD

1 GARLIC CLOVE, MINCED

$1 1/2$ TABLESPOONS RED WINE VINEGAR

SALT AND FRESHLY GROUND BLACK PEPPER

8 CUPS (16 OZ/480G) MIXED BABY SALAD GREENS

$1 1/2$ CUPS (5 OZ/150G) FINE, DRY BREAD CRUMBS

Cut each goat cheese round in half horizontally to make 6 discs total.

Warm 5 tablespoons ($2 1/2$ fl oz/75ml) of the olive oil in a saucepan. With the back of your chef's knife, tap the thyme, oregano, and rosemary sprigs to bruise the stems slightly. Add the herbs to the oil and remove the oil from the heat. Let the oil cool. Pour the oil over the goat cheese rounds, coating all sides with the oil. Let marinate for at least 2 hours, or up to 2 weeks in the refrigerator.

Preheat the oven to 325°F (160°C). Combine the bacon and bread and place on a baking sheet. Bake, tossing occasionally, until the bread and bacon are light golden, about 12 minutes. Increase the heat to 400°F (200°C).

In a small bowl, whisk the remaining 3 tablespoons ($1 1/2$ fl oz/45ml) olive oil, mustard, garlic, and red wine vinegar. Season with salt and pepper.

Season the bread crumbs with salt and pepper. Remove the goat cheese from the oil and coat with bread crumbs. Place on a baking sheet and bake until the cheese is warm in the center and bubbling around the edges, 4 to 6 minutes.

Toss the vinaigrette with the greens. Arrange some greens on each salad plate and place 1 cheese round in the center. Surround the cheese with croutons and bacon and serve immediately.

SERVES 6

NOTE: THIS CHEESE IS BEST WHEN MARINATED FOR AT LEAST 1 WEEK BEFORE USING. THE OIL CAN BE USED AGAIN.

Food doesn't get much better than warm, soft goat cheese, hot from the oven, spread on fresh bread, with a few salad greens and crisp bacon scattered around the edges.

Tomato and Herbed Ricotta Salata Salad

$^1/_2$ POUND (220G) RICOTTA SALATA
2 TABLESPOONS CHOPPED FRESH BASIL
2 TABLESPOONS CHOPPED FRESH CHIVES
1 TABLESPOON CHOPPED FRESH MINT
1 TEASPOON CHOPPED FRESH OREGANO
1 TEASPOON CHOPPED FRESH THYME
5 LARGE RIPE TOMATOES, CUT INTO $^1/_4$-INCH (0.6CM) SLICES
$^1/_2$ POUND (240G) ASSORTED CHERRY TOMATOES, RED, ORANGE,
    YELLOW PLUM, GREEN, HALVED
SALT
$^1/_4$ CUP (2 FL OZ/60ML) EXTRA-VIRGIN OLIVE OIL
3 TABLESPOONS (1$^1/_2$ FL OZ/45ML) BALSAMIC VINEGAR
FRESHLY GROUND BLACK PEPPER
BASIL, MINT, OREGANO, AND THYME SPRIGS AS A GARNISH

Forty million Americans grow tomatoes, a true testament that picking homegrown tomatoes, warm from the summer sun, is pure joy. Slice and combine them with herbs and ricotta salata, a salted and drained ricotta with a firmer, drier texture than the usual version. More than once, I have been told that this is someone's favorite dish.

Crumble the ricotta salata in a bowl. Add the basil, chives, mint, oregano, and thyme and mix together until all of the herbs stick to the crumbled cheese. Set aside.

Place the sliced tomatoes on a serving platter, overlapping slightly. Scatter the cherry tomatoes on top. Season with salt.

In a small bowl, whisk together the olive oil and vinegar. Season to taste with salt and pepper. Drizzle the vinaigrette onto the tomatoes and let sit for 10 minutes.

To serve, scatter the cheese over the tomatoes and garnish with basil, mint, oregano and thyme sprigs. Serve immediately.

SERVES 6

White Bean Salad with Peppers, Goat Cheese, and Mint

*T*his, with a bowl of gazpacho, is a meal in itself. A loaf of bread, a bottle of wine, a picnic table, and some sunshine and you have everything you need for a summer lunch in the vineyards.

1 CUP (7 OZ/210G) DRIED WHITE BEANS
6 TABLESPOONS (3 FL OZ/90ML) EXTRA-VIRGIN OLIVE OIL
5 TABLESPOONS 2^1/$_2$ FL OZ/75ML) RED WINE VINEGAR
SALT AND FRESHLY GROUND PEPPER
1 RED BELL PEPPER, CUT INTO ^{1}/$_4$-INCH (0.6CM) DICE
1 GREEN BELL PEPPER, CUT INTO ^{1}/$_4$-INCH (0.6CM) DICE
1 YELLOW BELL PEPPER, CUT INTO ^{1}/$_4$-INCH (0.6CM) DICE
1 SMALL RED ONION, CUT INTO ^{1}/$_4$-INCH (0.6CM) DICE
1 GARLIC CLOVE, MINCED
5 OUNCES (150G) FRESH GOAT CHEESE
^{1}/$_4$ CUP (^{1}/$_4$ OZ/8G) FRESH MINT LEAVES, CUT INTO THIN STRIPS

Pick over the beans and discard any stones or damaged ones. Cover with plenty of water and let soak for 4 hours. Place the beans in a saucepan with plenty of water over high heat and bring to a boil. Reduce the heat to low and simmer until skins just begin to crack and beans are tender, about 30 to 40 minutes. Drain the beans.

In the meantime, whisk together the olive oil and vinegar in a small bowl. Season to taste with salt and pepper. Add to the warm beans and let sit until the beans cool.

When the beans have cooled, add the diced peppers, onions, and garlic and mix well. Season with salt and pepper and additional vinegar if needed.

To serve place the beans in a serving bowl and crumble the cheese over the top. Garnish with mint and serve.

SERVES 6

Watercress and Beet Salad
with Gorgonzola and Walnuts

2 POUNDS (900G) MEDIUM BEETS, RED OR GOLD, WASHED

1/4 CUP (2 FL OZ/60ML) EXTRA-VIRGIN OLIVE OIL

2 1/2 TABLESPOONS (1 1/2 FL OZ/45ML) RED WINE VINEGAR

SALT AND FRESHLY GROUND BLACK PEPPER

1 SMALL HEAD RADICCHIO, TORN INTO 2-INCH (5-CM) PIECES

3 OUNCES (90G) GORGONZOLA CHEESE, CRUMBLED

1/2 CUP (2 1/2 OZ/75G) WALNUT HALVES, TOASTED (SEE NOTE)

1 1/2 CUPS (5 OZ/150G) LOOSELY PACKED WATERCRESS, STEMS TRIMMED

Preheat the oven to 375°F (190°C).

Place the beets in a shallow baking pan and drizzle with the oil and 1 tablespoon water. Roll the beets to coat with the oil. Season with salt and pepper, cover with aluminum foil, and bake until the beets are tender and can be easily pierced with a fork, 60 to 80 minutes, depending on the size of the beets. When the beets are tender, remove from the oven and let cool. Pour the oil from the bottom of the pan into a small bowl and reserve. When the beets are cool enough to handle, peel the beets and cut them into wedges.

In the meantime, whisk together the red wine vinegar and the reserved oil. Season to taste with salt and pepper. Toss all but 1 tablespoon of the vinaigrette with the beets and radicchio. Place the beets on a serving platter. Scatter the Gorgonzola and walnuts over the top. Toss the remaining 1 tablespoon of the vinaigrette with the watercress. Season with salt and pepper. Top the beets with the watercress and serve immediately.

SERVES 6

NOTE: TO TOAST WALNUTS OR PECANS, PLACE THEM ON A BAKING SHEET IN A 375°F (190°C) OVEN FOR 5 TO 7 MINUTES, UNTIL LIGHT GOLDEN AND HOT TO THE TOUCH.

Gorgonzola is one of Italy's most recognized cheeses, but it is also a metro stop outside of Milan, where the infamous cheese was made many years ago. Now it is produced all over Lombardy, far from the original site. In the United States, there are some excellent blue-veined cheeses being made, such as Maytag Blue from Iowa.

Warm Grilled Bread Salad
with Fresh Mozzarella

2 JAPANESE EGGPLANTS, SLICED ON THE DIAGONAL INTO $^1/_4$-INCH
    (0.6-CM) SLICES

5 TABLESPOONS ($2^1/_2$ FL OZ/75ML) EXTRA-VIRGIN OLIVE OIL

6 LARGE SLICES COARSE-TEXTURED COUNTRY-STYLE BREAD, CUT INTO
    APPROXIMATELY 2- TO $2^1/_2$-INCH (5- TO 7-CM) WEDGES

2 GARLIC CLOVES, PEELED

3 TABLESPOONS ($1^1/_2$ FL OZ/45ML) LEMON JUICE

4 ANCHOVY FILLETS, SOAKED IN COLD WATER FOR 10 MINUTES,
    PATTED DRY AND MASHED

1 SHALLOT, MINCED

SALT AND FRESHLY GROUND BLACK PEPPER

$^3/_4$ POUND (360G) FRESH COW'S MILK MOZZARELLA CHEESE, THINLY SLICED

6 LEMON WEDGES

12 BABY RADISHES WITH FRESH BRIGHT GREEN LEAVES

24 IMPORTED BLACK OLIVES

1 RECIPE ARTICHOKES STEWED WITH OLIVE OIL, LEMON, AND PLENTY OF
    GARLIC (SEE PAGE 49)

1 RED BELL PEPPER, ROASTED AND CUT INTO 1-INCH (2.5-CM) STRIPS
    (SEE PAGE 27)

1 YELLOW BELL PEPPER, ROASTED AND CUT INTO 1-INCH (2.5-CM) STRIPS

Preheat the oven to 375°F (190°C). Brush the eggplant with 1 tablespoon of the oil and place them in a single layer on a baking sheet. Bake on the top shelf of the oven, turning occasionally, until golden, 15 to 18 minutes. Set aside to cool.

Toast or grill the bread until golden and rub each side with garlic.

In a small bowl, whisk together the lemon juice, anchovies, shallots, and remaining 4 tablespoons (2 fl oz/60ml) olive oil. Season with salt and pepper.

Place the toasted or grilled bread in a single layer on a baking sheet and place the mozzarella on top, distributing evenly. Bake on the top shelf of the oven until the mozzarella begins to melt, 1 to 2 minutes.

To serve, place two pieces of grilled bread on each plate. Drizzle a spoonful of the anchovy-lemon sauce on top. Garnish with eggplant, lemon wedges, radishes, olives, artichokes, or roasted pepper strips and serve immediately.

SERVES 6

This is a cross between a salad and a crostini. It's colorful, bright, flavorful, and really healthy— everything a good dish should be, all wrapped into one. Serve it as a first course before grilled lamb chops or rib-eye steaks.

Soft Mozzarella
Poached with Tomatoes and Basil

$1/4$ CUP (2 FL OZ/60ML) EXTRA-VIRGIN OLIVE OIL

4 GARLIC CLOVES, CRUSHED

3 POUNDS (1.4KG) TOMATOES, PEELED, SEEDED, CHOPPED, AND DRAINED,
    FRESH OR CANNED

SALT AND FRESHLY GROUND BLACK PEPPER

6 SMALL BALLS FRESH BUFFALO MOZZARELLA CHEESE, ABOUT 3 OUNCES
    (90G) EACH, DRAINED, AT ROOM TEMPERATURE

$1/2$ CUP ($1/2$ OZ/15G) FRESH BASIL LEAVES

BASIL SPRIGS AS A GARNISH

CRUSTY BREAD

Heat the oil in a large saucepan over medium heat. Add the garlic
and cook, stirring, until the garlic is golden, about 2 minutes.
Remove the garlic and discard. Reduce the heat to medium low, add
the tomatoes, and simmer until the tomatoes soften and begin to
liquify. Season to taste with salt and pepper. Let cool for 10 minutes.
Puree in a blender until smooth.

Twenty minutes before serving, bring the sauce to a simmer in a
large saucepan over medium heat. Place the mozzarella in the sauce
so that it is half submerged. Remove the pan from the heat and let
sit 6 to 8 minutes.

In the meantime, cut the basil into thin strips. To serve, place a
piece of warm mozzarella on each plate. Stir the basil into the sauce.
Spoon the sauce around the mozzarella. Garnish with basil sprigs
and serve immediately, with bread.

SERVES 6

This is one of those dishes that may seem a bit odd, but after you've tried it once, I promise it will become a favorite. Imagine soft creamy mozzarella surrounded by a pool of sweet tomato sauce and basil. Serve it with plenty of crusty bread or bruschetta, toasted bread rubbed with garlic and drizzled with your best extra-virgin olive oil.

Yes, buffalo mozzarella is made from the milk of buffalos—water buffalos from southern Italy. It is a little more expensive than cow's milk mozzarella (called fior de latte in Italy) and must be purchased very fresh. If it's unavailable, try using cow's milk mozzarella, made and readily available in the United States. If the pieces of mozzarella you purchase are larger than 3 ounces (90g) each, cut them to the correct size.

Goat Cheese and Green Onion Galette

1¹/₂ CUPS (6 OZ/180G) ALL-PURPOSE WHITE FLOUR, CHILLED IN THE
   FREEZER FOR 1 HOUR
¹/₄ TEASPOON SALT
9 TABLESPOONS (4¹/₂ OZ/135G) BUTTER, CUT INTO ¹/₂-INCH (1.25-CM)
   PIECES, CHILLED IN THE FREEZER FOR 1 HOUR
¹/₃ TO ¹/₂ CUP (3 TO 4 OZ/85 TO 120ML) ICE WATER
1 TABLESPOON OLIVE OIL
2 BUNCHES GREEN ONIONS, WHITE AND GREEN, THINLY SLICED
5 OUNCES (150G) GOAT CHEESE
4 OUNCES (120G) RICOTTA CHEESE
³/₄ CUP (3 OZ/90G) COARSELY GRATED MOZZARELLA CHEESE
¹/₄ CUP (2 FL OZ/60ML) CRÈME FRAÎCHE
¹/₄ CUP (1 OZ/30G) GRATED PARMIGIANO REGGIANO CHEESE
SALT AND FRESHLY GROUND BLACK PEPPER

A galette is a fancy way of saying a thin pie. This one has a crunchy crisp dough, rich with butter. It is a perfect casing for creamy hot ricotta, crème fraîche, mozzarella, green onions, and a bit of Parmigiano. This has been one of my all-time favorites for years. You'll see why! Serve it with a full-bodied Chardonnay.

Place the flour and salt on a cold work surface. With a pastry scraper, cut the butter into the flour until half is the size of peas and the other half a little larger. Make a well in the center and add half of the ice water. Push together with your fingertips and set aside any dough that holds together. Add the rest of the water and repeat. Form the mixture into a rough ball. Alternately this can be made in the an electric mixer using the same technique. Roll out the dough on a well-floured surface into a 14-inch (35-cm) circle and trim the edges. Place on a large sheet pan in the refrigerator.

Warm the olive oil in a large skillet over medium heat. Add the green onions and cook until soft, 4 to 5 minutes. Remove from the heat and let cool.

Mix together the green onions, goat cheese, ricotta, mozzarella, crème fraîche, and Parmigiano. Mix well and season with salt and pepper.

Preheat the oven to 375°F (190°C). Remove the pastry from the refrigerator. Spread the cheese over the pastry, leaving a 2¹/₂-inch (6.5-cm) border around the edge uncovered. Fold the uncovered edge of the pastry over the cheese, pleating it to make it fit. There will be an open hole in the center revealing the filling. Bake the galette in the oven for 35 to 40 minutes, until golden brown. Let cool for 5 minutes, then slide the galette off the pan and onto a serving plate. Serve hot, warm, or at room temperature.

SERVES 6

*T*he most famous version of pecorino, an aged sheep's milk cheese, is Pecorino Romano, the one we've all been using in the United States for ages. At one point, the only pecorino available was from Italy. Finally, we are making some terrific pecorino in the United States. Besides grating it and putting it on pasta with your favorite tomato sauce or in pesto, you can shave it into thin shards and toss it into a salad.

Fennel, Arugula, and Radicchio Salad with Shaved Pecorino

2 MEDIUM FENNEL BULBS, TRIMMED
1 SMALL HEAD RADICCHIO, LEAVES SEPARATED AND TORN INTO 2-INCH (5-CM) PIECES
2 BUNCHES ARUGULA, STEMS REMOVED
12 SMALL RADISHES, THINLY SLICED
$1/4$ CUP (2 FL OZ/60ML) EXTRA-VIRGIN OLIVE OIL
2 TABLESPOONS WHITE WINE VINEGAR
1 SHALLOT, MINCED
1 GARLIC CLOVE, MINCED
SALT AND FRESHLY GROUND BLACK PEPPER
3-OUNCE (90G) CHUNK PECORINO CHEESE, SHAVED INTO THIN SLICES
1 BUNCH BABY RADISHES WITH FRESH, BRIGHT GREEN LEAVES

With a sharp knife, a mandoline, or an electric meat slicer, shave the fennel into paper-thin slices. Place in a large bowl with the radicchio, arugula, and radishes.

For the vinaigrette, whisk the olive oil, vinegar, shallot, and garlic together in a small bowl. Season with salt and pepper.

To serve, toss the vinaigrette with the fennel, radicchio, arugula, and radishes. Place on a platter and scatter the shaved pecorino over the top. Garnish with the baby radishes and serve immediately.

SERVES 6

*S*tart this recipe by buying the best quality fresh mozzarella cheese you can find—even buffalo milk mozzarella, if you can find and afford it! Cut it into cubes and, just before serving, add the mozzarella to the hot pasta and sauce. As you serve the dish, the cheese starts to melt together with the tomatoes. Talk about "melting in your mouth!"

Farfalle with Olives, Capers, Tomatoes, and Mozzarella

$1/4$ CUP (2 FL OZ/60ML) EXTRA-VIRGIN OLIVE OIL
6 LARGE TOMATOES, PEELED, SEEDED, DICED, AND DRAINED, ABOUT 3 POUNDS (1.4KG)
3 TABLESPOONS (1 OZ/30G) CAPERS
$3/4$ CUP ($4 1/2$ OZ/135G) ASSORTED IMPORTED OLIVES, PITTED AND COARSELY CHOPPED
SALT AND FRESHLY GROUND BLACK PEPPER
1 POUND (450G) FARFALLE
$3/4$ CUP (1 OZ/30G) FRESH BASIL LEAVES
$3/4$ POUND (350G) FRESH MOZZARELLA CHEESE, DICED

Heat the olive oil in a large skillet over medium-high heat. Add the tomatoes and cook until soft, about 10 minutes. Add the capers and olives and stir together. Season to taste with salt and pepper. Remove the pan from the heat and reserve.

Bring a large pot of salted water to a boil. Add the pasta and cook until al dente, 10 to 12 minutes or according to the directions on the package. In the meantime, heat the tomato mixture until hot, about 1 minute. Cut the basil into thin strips. When the pasta is done, drain and add the tomato sauce. Stir in the mozzarella and basil and serve immediately.

SERVES 6

Linguine with Goat Cheese and Arugula

1/4 CUP (2 FL OZ/60ML) OLIVE OIL
5 OUNCES (150G) PANCETTA, DICED
1 GARLIC CLOVE, MINCED
1/2 CUP (4 FL OZ/120ML) HEAVY CREAM
8 OUNCES (240G) FRESH GOAT CHEESE
1/4 CUP (1/4 OZ/8G) FRESH SNIPPED CHIVES
1/4 TEASPOON CRUSHED RED PEPPER FLAKES
SALT AND FRESHLY GROUND BLACK PEPPER
12 OUNCES (350G) LINGUINE
11/4 CUPS (5 OZ/150G) GRATED PARMIGIANO REGGIANO CHEESE
4 CUPS (1 LB/450G) ARUGULA, STEMS REMOVED, VERY COARSELY CHOPPED

Warm the olive oil in a large skillet over medium-low heat. Add the pancetta and cook until light golden, 10 to 15 minutes. Remove the mixture from the pan, place in a bowl, and let cool. Add the garlic, heavy cream, goat cheese, chives, and crushed red pepper flakes and mash together. Season to taste with salt and pepper. Set aside.

Bring a large pot of salted water to a boil. Add the pasta and cook until al dente, 7 to 9 minutes or according to the directions on the package. Drain the pasta, reserving 2 tablespoons of pasta water. Toss the hot pasta, pasta water, and half the Parmigiano with the goat cheese mixture. Coat the pasta well with the sauce. Add the arugula and toss together. Place on a platter, garnish with the remaining Parmigiano, and serve immediately.

SERVES 6

Chèvre means goat in French, but in the United States the word means goat cheese. Widespread enthusiasm for chèvre, which has been building for the last several years, has created substantial growth in the American goat-cheese industry, especially as a cottage industry. Surprisingly, goat cheese is being made in nearly every state in the United States. Tart and tangy goat cheese makes a luscious creamy sauce for pasta tossed with pancetta, garlic, crushed red pepper flakes, and fresh arugula. Be careful—this dish is addictive when served with a dry Sauvignon Blanc.

Lasagne with Wild Mushrooms, Leeks, and Gorgonzola

My mother has always had the knack for making great lasagne. If pressed, she would even say it was one of her best dishes. But she always made it the traditional way with tomato sauce, lots of mozzarella, and ricotta. Here, I have replaced the tomatoes with wild mushrooms, leeks, and a creamy béchamel with Gorgonzola. If wild mushrooms are unavailable, substitute button or other cultivated mushrooms.

$^{1}/_{2}$ POUND (225G) DRY LASAGNE NOODLES
SALT AND FRESHLY GROUND BLACK PEPPER
15 OUNCES (425G) RICOTTA CHEESE
$^{3}/_{4}$ CUP (3 OZ/90G) FRESHLY GRATED PARMIGIANO REGGIANO CHEESE
4 TABLESPOONS (2 FL OZ/60ML) EXTRA-VIRGIN OLIVE OIL
5 LARGE LEEKS, WHITE PLUS 3 INCHES (7.5CM) OF THE GREEN, CUT INTO 1-INCH (2.5-CM) DICE
$1^{1}/_{2}$ POUNDS WILD MUSHROOMS, THINLY SLICED
5 GARLIC CLOVES, MINCED
4 TABLESPOONS (2 OZ/60G) UNSALTED BUTTER
$4^{1}/_{2}$ TABLESPOONS ($1^{1}/_{4}$ OZ/35G) FLOUR
$3^{1}/_{2}$ CUPS (28 FL OZ/825ML) WHOLE MILK
6 OUNCES (180G) GORGONZOLA, STILTON, OR ROQUEFORT CHEESE
FRESHLY GRATED NUTMEG
4 OUNCES (120G) WHOLE-MILK MOZZARELLA CHEESE, COARSELY GRATED

Bring a large pot of salted water to a boil. Add the lasagne noodles and cook until al dente, 8 to 12 minutes or according to the directions on the package. While the pasta is cooking, fill a large bowl with cold water. When the pasta is done, drain the pasta and place in the bowl of water to cool. After 5 minutes, drain the pasta and place the pieces in a single layer on a baking sheet. Cover with plastic wrap and set aside.

In a small bowl mix together the ricotta, Parmigiano, and salt and pepper. Set aside.

Heat 2 tablespoons of the olive oil in a skillet over medium-low heat. Add the leeks and cook uncovered, stirring occasionally, until the leeks are very soft and light golden, about 30 minutes. Remove the leeks from the pan and reserve.

Heat the remaining 2 tablespoons olive oil in a large skillet. Add the mushrooms and cook until they are soft and the liquid has evaporated, 7 to 10 minutes. Add the garlic and stir over the heat for 1 minute. Add to the leeks and stir together.

Melt the butter in a saucepan over medium-high heat. Stir in the flour and cook, uncovered, stirring constantly for 2 to 3 minutes. Add the milk and whisk constantly until it comes back to a boil and thickens, 4 to 5 minutes. Add the Gorgonzola and stir until smooth. Season with salt, pepper, and nutmeg.

Preheat the oven to 375°F (190°C). Oil a 13- x 9-inch (33 x 23-cm) baking dish. Cover the bottom of the baking dish with a single layer of pasta. Cover the pasta with one-third of the ricotta mixture. Sprinkle one-third of mushroom and leek mixture over the ricotta. Spread one-third of the sauce over the vegetables. Repeat with the remaining 2 layers. Sprinkle the mozzarella evenly over the top layer. Bake on the top shelf of the oven until the top is golden and bubbling around the edges, 40 to 50 minutes. Remove from the oven and let stand 15 minutes before serving.

SERVES 8 TO 10

Focaccia with Creamy Taleggio

2 TEASPOONS ACTIVE DRY YEAST
$^1/_4$ CUP (2 FL OZ/60ML) PLUS 1 CUP (8 FL OZ/240ML) WARM (110°F/43°C)
    WATER
3 TABLESPOONS ($1^1/_2$ FL OZ/45ML) EXTRA-VIRGIN OLIVE OIL
3 CUPS (12 OZ/350G) UNBLEACHED BREAD FLOUR
SALT
12 OUNCES (350G) TALEGGIO CHEESE, COARSELY GRATED
$^1/_3$ CUP ($1^1/_2$ OZ/45G) FINELY GRATED AGED PECORINO CHEESE

Whisk together the yeast and $^1/_4$ cup (2 fl oz/60ml) water and let sit until creamy, about 20 minutes. Add the remaining 1 cup (8 fl oz/240ml) water, the olive oil, flour, and $^1/_2$ teaspoon salt. Knead on a lightly floured surface until smooth and soft, 7 to 8 minutes. Place in a well-oiled bowl and turn the dough over to coat the dough. Cover with plastic wrap and let rise in a warm place (75°F/24°C) until it doubles in volume, about $1^1/_2$ hours.

Place a pizza stone or tiles on the bottom shelf of the oven. Heat the oven to 500°F (260°C) for at least 30 minutes.

Divide the dough into 4 pieces and form each piece into a round ball. On a well-floured surface, roll 1 piece of dough at a time into a 9-inch (23-cm) circle, $^1/_8$-inch (0.3cm) thick. Transfer 1 piece to a well-floured pizza peel or paddle. In a bowl mix together the Taleggio and pecorino. Spread one-third of the cheese mixture on the dough, leaving a 1-inch border. Brush the edges of the dough lightly with water. Roll another ball to the same size and place on top. Crimp the edges to seal well. Pinch a hole in the second piece of dough in the center.

Bake the focaccia on the hot stone until light golden and crisp, 7 to 10 minutes. Repeat with the remaining dough and cheese filling, making 1 more focaccia. Serve immediately.

MAKES 2 FOCACCIE AND SERVES 10

I drove what seemed like a million miles out of my way to taste this flatbread in the village of Recco on the Ligurian Coast of northern Italy. After the chef crimped and sealed the edges of this two-crusted pizza, he deliberately tore a hole into the top to keep the pie from expanding like a football when baked. The pie was brought to my table, hot from the stone oven, and I realized my trip was well worth it. Now you can make this delicious pie right at home—you don't even have to buy a plane ticket to Italy. Serve with a Sangiovese or a Pinot Noir.

Homemade Ricotta and Mint Ravioli with Sweet Tomatoes

These melt-in-your-mouth ravioli are a bit of an effort to make, but once you have the gist, you won't soon forget or regret learning the skill of ravioli-making. Make them well in advance and freeze them. When you have the urge for ravioli, presto—out of the freezer and directly into boiling water.

1 POUND (450G) FRESH SPINACH, WASHED AND DRIED

3 OUNCES (90G) MASCARPONE CHEESE

3 OUNCES (90G) RICOTTA CHEESE

1 CUP (4 OZ/120G) GRATED PARMIGIANO REGGIANO CHEESE

1 EGG YOLK

1 SMALL GARLIC CLOVE, MINCED

1 TABLESPOON CHOPPED FRESH MINT

SALT AND FRESHLY GROUND BLACK PEPPER

LARGE PINCH OF FRESHLY GRATED NUTMEG

1 RECIPE EGG PASTA DOUGH (SEE NEXT PAGE)

3 TABLESPOONS (1^1/$_2$ FL OZ/45ML) EXTRA-VIRGIN OLIVE OIL

5 WHOLE GARLIC CLOVES, PEELED AND BRUISED

4 CUPS (2 LB/900G) PEELED, SEEDED, AND CHOPPED TOMATOES, FRESH OR CANNED

^{1}/$_3$ CUP (^{1}/$_2$ OZ/15G) FRESH BASIL LEAVES

Heat a large skillet over medium heat. Wilt the spinach, tossing continuously. Place the spinach on paper towels and press to remove all moisture. Chop the spinach and place in a large bowl. Add the mascarpone, ricotta, ^{1}/$_3$ cup (1^1/$_2$ oz/45g) of the Parmigiano, the egg yolks, garlic, and mint, and mix well. Season to taste with salt, pepper, and nutmeg. Place in the refrigerator until needed.

Divide the dough into 4 pieces. By machine or by hand, roll the pasta ^{1}/8-inch (0.3-cm) thick. Place a pasta sheet on a lightly floured work surface. Spoon mounds of the cheese filling onto the sheet just below the center, spacing them about 2 to 2 ^{1}/2 inches (5 to 6cm) apart. With a spray mister filled with water, lightly mist around the mounds of filling. Roll the second sheet and place it over the first, matching the edges. Press around the edges and mounds of filling to seal. Using a fluted cutting wheel, cut between the filling and the edges to form 4-inch (10-cm) squares. Place them in a single layer on a well-floured baking sheet.

Heat the olive oil in a large skillet over medium-high heat. Add the whole garlic cloves and cook until golden, 2 to 3 minutes. Remove and discard them. Add the tomatoes to the pan and let cook until the tomatoes are soft, 5 to 10 minutes. Season to taste with salt and pepper and cook until half of the liquid has evaporated, about 10 minutes.

Bring a large pot of salted water to a boil. Add the ravioli and cook until al dente, 3 to 4 minutes. Drain and place in a bowl. Add the tomato sauce and gently mix together. Place on a platter and sprinkle with the remaining $2/3$ cup ($2^1/2$ oz/75g) Parmigiano and the basil leaves.

MAKES ABOUT 32 LARGE RAVIOLI AND SERVES 6

Egg Pasta Dough

2 CUPS (8 OZ/240G) ALL-PURPOSE FLOUR
SALT
2 WHOLE EGGS

In the bowl of the food processor, pulse together the flour and $1/4$ teaspoon salt. Add the eggs and 2 tablespoons of water and process until the dough forms a soft ball but is not sticky. If so, add more flour 1 tablespoon at a time until it isn't sticky. If it is dry, add additional water 1 tablespoon at a time. Remove the dough from the food processor bowl and knead on a very lightly floured board until soft and smooth, 2 to 3 minutes. Wrap the dough in plastic wrap and place in the refrigerator for 30 minutes or up to one day to rest before using.

MAKES APPROXIMATELY 1 POUND (450G) PASTA

A *few years ago,* my architect husband, Paul, and I decided to remodel our kitchen. Think about it: an architect and a food writer with a background in Fine Arts talking about kitchen design. Can you imagine the heated discussions?

We started by converting what had been a fireplace into a Tuscan oven, where I could grill and spit-roast meats right in the kitchen. Then Paul came up with the idea of a wood-fired brick oven for baking pizza. I almost let him talk me into it, but then I realized that with a conventional oven and a convection oven, a fourth oven might be overkill.

But here's my point: We live in an era and a part of the world in which specialty ovens, artisanal baking, and fantastic old-world breads have become a part of everyday life. I'm delighted. And I'm on a crusade to remind the world that these "upscale" breads aren't just some kind of yuppie fad. They're

what much of the world has been baking and eating for thousands of years.

Take the wood-fired brick oven, for example. There's a long-standing tradition throughout Europe of village bakers whose brick ovens supply bread for an entire community or neighborhood. In rural areas, farmers often build brick ovens and bake bread to supplement their income between harvests.

I remember when Chez Panisse Café installed a wood-burning pizza oven in the upstairs café in the early 1980s. Believe it or not, at that time, it was one of only a handful of wood-fired ovens America. People loved the café's open kitchen, where they could watch the Italian pizza chef, Michele, as he deftly maneuvered the pizzas, rotating and repositioning them with a long wooden peel, his face shining in the fiery glow of the oven. And they loved his crisp-crusted, golden pizzas and focaccias, glistening with olive oil and bits of fresh tomato. Who had ever thought pizza could taste so heavenly?

Nowadays, wood-fired ovens are everywhere. In fact, they're practically a restaurant cliché. But that's okay with me, because they've brought with

Oven

The wood-fired oven at Bay Village Bakers in Point Reyes Station, California.
Opposite: Country-style bread at Bay Village Bakers.

them a whole movement of artisanal baking that's putting fresh, simple, lovingly prepared breads on our tables.

That was the impulse behind Bay Village Bakers in the tiny Northern California town of Point Reyes Station. When Chad Robertson and Elizabeth Prueitt built a wood-fired oven in a shed behind their house, their dream was to provide hearty, country-style bread for their neighbors. Now they're doing just that.

I spent a day baking with Chad, and came away amazed at how simple—and how surprisingly subtle—the art of baking bread can be. Chad starts a fresh fire in the baking chamber of his traditional Roman-style oven in the early afternoon, letting it burn slowly for about six hours. By the time he's ready to go to sleep, the fire has died down and he closes the oven for the night. In the morning, the warmth of the fire has permeated the bricks, creating an even, dry heat that's ideal for bread-baking. The design of the oven is so efficient that it can hold a temperature of 600–700° F (300–370° C) just from that one firing.

Instead of using commercial yeast, Chad does

what artisanal bakers have done for more than five thousand years: He makes his own starter by fermenting flour and water. Each day, he mixes the starter with more flour, water, and a little sea salt in a traditional wooden trough. The dough is kneaded and allowed to rise for about six hours before it's shaped by hand into rounds and short, country-style baguettes and given a second rising overnight. The loaves are scored with Chad's signature mark— every baker has his own— and baked in small batches throughout the next day.

What surprised me most about the day that I spent at Bay Village Bakers was how low-tech the process is. There are no gas jets, no fancy equipment, no mysterious ingredients. To me, that says something really inspiring. Flour, water, salt, and heat are all it takes to make bread that's as good as anything you can imagine. But you also need the human element: hands to work the dough, eyes to watch it rise and brown, a nose to sense the moment when the baking is done, and happy mouths to taste the baker's art.

Various shapes of bread set aside for their final rising at Bay Village Bakers.

Italian Bread Salad with Tomatoes and Basil

1/2 POUND (225G) COARSE-TEXTURED COUNTRY-STYLE BREAD,
   3 TO 4 DAYS OLD
1 MEDIUM HOT-HOUSE CUCUMBER, PEELED, SEEDED, AND CUT INTO
   1/2-INCH (1.25-CM) DICE
SALT
5 MEDIUM RIPE TOMATOES, SEEDED AND DICED, ABOUT 1 1/2 TO 2 POUNDS
   (700 TO 900G)
1 MEDIUM RED ONION, DICED
1/2 CUP (1/2 OZ/15G) FRESH BASIL LEAVES
5 TABLESPOONS (2 1/2 FL OZ/75ML) RED WINE VINEGAR
2 GARLIC CLOVES, MINCED
1/3 CUP (3 FL OZ/80ML) EXTRA-VIRGIN OLIVE OIL
FRESHLY GROUND BLACK PEPPER

Slice the bread into 1-inch (2.5-cm) slices. Sprinkle the bread with
1/2 cup (4 fl oz/120ml) water and let sit for 2 minutes. Carefully squeeze
the bread until dry. Tear bread into rough 1-inch (2.5-cm) shapes and
let rest on paper towels, 20 minutes.

In the meantime, place the cucumbers on another few sheets of paper
towels. Sprinkle with salt and let rest 20 minutes. Place in a colander
and rinse with cold water. Dry on paper towels.

In a bowl, combine the cucumbers, tomatoes, and onions. Tear the basil
into 1/2 inch (1.25 cm) pieces and add to the vegetables. Add the bread
and toss carefully.

In a small bowl, whisk together the vinegar, garlic, and olive oil. Season
with salt and pepper. Carefully toss with the vegetables and bread and
set aside for 20 minutes. Place on a platter and serve.

SERVES 6

*Imagine a sandwich made
with the sweetest tomatoes and
fresh basil from the garden.
Now, tear up the bread, toss
it with the tomatoes, basil,
crisp cucumbers, red onions,
and a red wine vinaigrette.
What you have is panzanella,
a summertime staple from
Tuscany. It's become a staple
in my weekend wine-country
home as well.*

Parmigiano and Black Peppercorn Breadsticks

Most Americans think of breadsticks as tasteless pencil-like sticks of toast wrapped in waxy envelopes and served with antipasti at tacky Italian restaurants. But when homemade breadsticks are flavored with Parmigiano and a good dose of coarsely cracked black peppercorns and served hot from the oven, there's no comparison. Serve them simply with drinks or as an accompaniment to soups, salads, or, of course, a platter of antipasti.

2 TEASPOONS ACTIVE DRY YEAST
$3^1/_2$ CUPS (14 OZ/400G) UNBLEACHED BREAD FLOUR
$1^1/_2$ CUPS (12 FL OZ/350ML) LUKEWARM WATER, ABOUT 110°F (43°C)
2 TEASPOONS SALT
$2^1/_2$ TABLESPOONS COARSELY GROUND BLACK PEPPER
$^1/_4$ TEASPOON CAYENNE
2 TABLESPOONS EXTRA-VIRGIN OLIVE OIL
1 CUP (4 OZ/120G) FINELY GRATED PARMIGIANO REGGIANO CHEESE
$^1/_2$ CUP (2 OZ/60G) SEMOLINA

In a bowl, stir together the yeast, $^1/_2$ cup (2 oz/60g) of the flour, and $^1/_2$ cup (4 fl oz/120ml) warm water. Let stand until the mixture bubbles and rises slightly, 30 minutes. Add the remaining 3 cups flour, 1 cup (8 fl oz/240ml) warm water, the salt, pepper, cayenne, and olive oil, and stir together to form a ball. Knead on a lightly floured surface, kneading in the Parmigiano gradually, until smooth and elastic, 7 to 10 minutes. Alternately this can be made in an electric mixer on slow speed using the dough hook, kneading for 5 minutes.

Using your hands, shape the dough into an 15- x 5-inch (38- x 13-cm) rectangle. Brush with oil, cover loosely with plastic wrap, and let rise in a warm place, about 75°F (24°C), until doubled in volume, 1 to $1^1/_4$ hours.

Place a pizza stone on the bottom shelf of the oven and preheat to 450°F (230°C).

Sprinkle both sides of the dough with the semolina. Cut the dough into 5 equal 1-inch (2.5-cm) strips in the long direction. Cut the dough crosswise into 5 sections. This will make 25 pieces. Pick up each piece of dough and roll and stretch to fit the width of a baking sheet, about 8 to 10 inches long. Place in a single layer, 1 inch (2.5cm) apart, on an oiled baking sheet. Bake in the middle shelf of the oven until light golden, 10 to 12 minutes. Remove the breadsticks from the baking sheet and place directly onto the baking stone and bake until golden and crisp, 3 to 5 minutes. Remove from the oven and cool on a cooling rack.

MAKES 25 BREADSTICKS

Grilled Bread with Ripe Tomatoes and Olive Oil

2 GARLIC CLOVES, PEELED

SALT

$^1/_4$ CUP (2 FL OZ/60ML) EXTRA-VIRGIN OLIVE OIL

12 SLICES COARSE-TEXTURED COUNTRY-STYLE BREAD, $^3/_4$-INCH THICK

3 VERY RIPE TOMATOES

FRESHLY GROUND BLACK PEPPER

FOR THE OPTIONAL GARNISH

12 ANCHOVY FILLETS, SOAKED IN COLD WATER FOR 10 MINUTES AND
    PATTED DRY

6 PAPER-THIN SLICES SERRANO HAM OR PROSCIUTTO

12 PAPER-THIN SLICES MANCHEGO CHEESE

$^1/_2$ CUP (3 OZ/90G) GREEN OR BLACK IMPORTED OLIVES

Preheat a broiler or start a charcoal or wood fire.

Mash the garlic and a pinch of salt in a mortar and pestle and mix with the oil.

Grill the bread until golden brown.

Cut the tomatoes in half and, cupping the tomato in your palm with the cut side facing away from your palm, rub both sides of the toast with the tomato, squeezing slightly as you go along to leave pulp, seeds, and juice.

Drizzle the olive oil on each side and sprinkle with salt and pepper. Place on a platter and garnish with anchovies, Serrano ham, and Manchego cheese, placing the ham, Manchego, and anchovies alternately on top of the bread. Scatter the olives between the pieces of bread and serve.

SERVES 6

Picture this—thick slices of country-style bread toasted over a wood fire until lightly golden. Next, half a tomato is smeared all over the toast, leaving the seeds, sweet juice, and pulp. Drizzle with garlic-scented oil and you have the best of summer, a favorite in Barcelona and at my house in Napa when I need a spur-of-the-moment appetizer to serve with wine before dinner.

Crispy Cracker Bread

3 cups (12 oz/350g) unbleached bread flour
1 1/2 cups (6 oz/180g) fine semolina flour
Salt
1 1/2 to 1 3/4 cups (12 to 14 fl oz/350 to 400ml) lukewarm water
(110°f/76°c)
2 teaspoons fresh rosemary needles, optional
Coarse salt, optional

W hen I heard about the paper-thin, unleavened, crisp bread that Sardinia is famous for, I instantly headed in that direction. The first night, I was greeted with a big basket stacked with bread, the thinnest, crispiest bread I'd ever seen. It was shiny with Sardinian olive oil and scattered with rosemary needles. Carta di musica, or music-paper bread, it gets its name from being so thin, you can read sheet music through it. To taste carta di musi-ca, a trek to Sardinia may seem like a long way to go. So here is a recipe that I never dreamed would be so easy to reproduce at home.

In a bowl mix together the flour, semolina, and 1 1/2 teaspoons salt. Add the water slowly to form a ball, making sure that the dough isn't too sticky or elastic. If the dough is sticky, dust it with flour. Divide the dough into 15 equal pieces. Form them into small balls without working them too much and place on a floured baking sheet. Cover with plastic wrap and set aside in a warm place for 30 minutes.

Preheat the oven to 400°f (200°c). Place a pizza stone on the bottom shelf of the oven and heat for at least 30 minutes.

Place 1 piece of dough on a floured surface. Flatten with the palm of your hand. Dust the top with flour. With a rolling pin, roll the dough to a very thin circle, 8 to 10 inches in diameter and less than 1/16-inch (0.2-cm) thick. Place one at a time on a pizza peel and transfer to the baking stone. Bake until it begins to blister, 2 to 3 minutes. Turn the bread over and continue to bake until it is golden and crisp, about 2 minutes. Watch the bread closely, because it burns quickly. Cool on a rack and continue to bake the remaining breads. Sprinkle with rosemary and coarse salt if desired.

Serve warm in a large basket.

Makes 15 large breads and serves 8

Flatbread with Roasted Shallots and Garlic

FOR THE DOUGH
2¹/₂ TEASPOONS ACTIVE DRY YEAST
2¹/₂ CUPS (10 OZ/300G) UNBLEACHED BREAD FLOUR
1 CUP (8 FL OZ/240ML) WARM POTATO WATER (110°F/76°C)
¹/₄ CUP (2 FL OZ/60ML) EXTRA-VIRGIN OLIVE OIL
1 TEASPOON CHOPPED FRESH ROSEMARY
SALT

FOR THE TOPPING
2 TABLESPOONS EXTRA-VIRGIN OLIVE OIL
25 SMALL SHALLOTS, PEELED
20 GARLIC CLOVES, PEELED
2 TABLESPOONS SUGAR
3 CUPS (24 FL OZ/700ML) DRY RED WINE, SUCH AS CABERNET SAUVIGNON
COARSE SALT AND FRESHLY GROUND BLACK PEPPER

The potato water called for in the recipe is the water left after boiling peeled and quartered russet potatoes. Drain and mash the potatoes for dinner or use for another purpose, and reserve the water.

In a large bowl, mix the yeast, ¹/₂ cup of the flour, and ¹/₂ cup warm potato water. Let stand until the mixture bubbles up, about 30 minutes. Add the remaining 2 cups flour, ¹/₂ cup potato water, the olive oil, rosemary, and 1 teaspoon salt. Mix the dough thoroughly and knead on a floured board until soft yet still moist, 7 to 8 minutes. Place dough in an oiled bowl, turning once. Cover the bowl with plastic and set aside in a warm place, 75°F (00°C). Let rise 1 to 1¹/₂ hours until doubled in volume.

For the topping, heat the olive oil in a large skillet over medium-high heat. Add the shallots and garlic and cook uncovered, stirring occasionally, until the shallots are golden brown, about 10 minutes. Add the sugar, stir well, and cook until the sugar caramelizes, about 4 minutes. Add 2 cups of the wine, cover, and simmer over low heat until the onions are soft, 20 to 25 minutes. Remove the cover, add the remaining wine, and continue to simmer until the wine has evaporated, 10 to 15 minutes. Season with salt and pepper. Let the mixture cool.

Thirty minutes before baking, preheat a pizza stone on the bottom shelf of the oven to 500°F (260°C).

Form the dough into a round ball. Let rest for 5 minutes. On a floured surface, roll the dough into a 9- x 12-inch (23- x 30-cm) oval, ¹/₂-inch (1.25-cm) thick. Place on a well-floured pizza peel. Distribute the shallots and garlic on the top of the flatbread and press them into the dough slightly. Sprinkle with coarse salt. Transfer the flatbread directly onto the pizza stone and bake until golden brown and crisp, 12 to 15 minutes.

MAKES 1 FLATBREAD AND SERVES 6

Pizza with Shrimp and Spicy Hot Garlic Mayonnaise

1 RECIPE PIZZA DOUGH (SEE PAGE 107)

2 TABLESPOONS EXTRA-VIRGIN OLIVE OIL

$^{1}/_{4}$ TEASPOON CRUSHED RED PEPPER FLAKES

2 GARLIC CLOVES, MINCED

$^{3}/_{4}$ CUP (3 OZ/90G) COARSELY GRATED FONTINA CHEESE

$^{3}/_{4}$ CUP (3 OZ/90G) COARSELY GRATED MOZZARELLA CHEESE

$^{1}/_{3}$ RECIPE HOMEMADE OR PREPARED MAYONNAISE (SEE PAGE 52)

$^{1}/_{4}$ CUP (2 FL OZ/60ML) LEMON JUICE

SALT AND FRESHLY GROUND BLACK PEPPER

$^{1}/_{2}$ SMALL RED ONION, VERY THINLY SLICED

5 OUNCES (150G) PEELED MEDIUM SHRIMP, CUT IN HALF THE LONG WAY

1 TABLESPOON FRESH MINCED GREEN ONIONS OR CHIVES

Make the pizza dough and let rise.

Thirty minutes before baking, place a pizza stone or unglazed quarry tiles on the bottom shelf of the oven and set the oven temperature to 500°F (260°C).

Combine the olive oil, crushed red pepper flakes, and half of the garlic. Let stand for 30 minutes. In a bowl, combine the fontina and mozzarella and set aside.

Whisk the mayonnaise with the remaining garlic and lemon juice. Season to taste with salt and pepper. Whisk in 1 to 2 tablespoons water to make the mayonnaise a pourable consistency. Reserve in the refrigerator.

Punch down the dough. On a floured surface, divide the dough into 2 pieces and form into round balls. Roll 1 piece into a 9-inch (23-cm) circle, $^{1}/_{4}$-inch (0.6-cm) thick. Transfer it to a well-floured pizza peel or paddle. Brush the dough to within $^{1}/_{2}$ inch (1.25 cm) of the edge with the garlic-infused oil. Sprinkle the cheese mixture over the dough. Top with half of the onions, distributing evenly. Slide the pizza onto the pizza stone and bake until the edges just start to turn golden, 3 to 4 minutes. Remove the pizza from the oven, top with the shrimp, distributing evenly in a single layer, and continue to bake until the pizza is golden and crisp and the shrimp have curled, 5 to 8 minutes. Drizzle with half of the mayonnaise and serve immediately garnished with green onions or chives.

Make a second pizza with the remaining ingredients.

MAKES 2 PIZZAS, 9 INCHES (23CM) IN DIAMETER

The great thing about pizzas is they are so versatile. You can top them with just about any flavor combination. With this one, I bake the pizza with shrimp. After it is cooked, I drizzle the top with garlic mayonnaise and watch it melt. I have also made this pizza with rings of fresh calamari with equally delicious results. Serve with a dry Sauvignon Blanc.

Pizza with Arugula and Shaved Parmigiano

1 RECIPE PIZZA DOUGH (SEE PAGE 107)
2 GARLIC CLOVES, MINCED
4 TABLESPOONS (2 FL OZ/60ML) EXTRA-VIRGIN OLIVE OIL
$^3/_4$ CUP (3 OZ/90G) COARSELY GRATED MOZZARELLA CHEESE
$^3/_4$ CUP (3 OZ/90G) COARSELY GRATED FONTINA CHEESE
1 TABLESPOON LEMON JUICE
SALT AND FRESHLY GROUND BLACK PEPPER
2 LARGE BUNCHES OF ARUGULA, ENDS TRIMMED
6-OUNCE (180-G) CHUNK PARMIGIANO REGGIANO CHEESE

ere is another hot-from-the-oven pizza topped with a cool salad. On this one, for a variation, try adding a few paper-thin slices of prosciutto.

Make the pizza dough and let rise.

Thirty minutes before baking, place a pizza stone or unglazed quarry tiles on the bottom shelf of the oven and set the oven temperature to 500°F (260°C).

Combine half of the garlic and 2 tablespoons of the olive oil and let stand for 30 minutes. In a bowl, combine the fontina and mozzarella and set aside.

For the vinaigrette, whisk together the remaining 2 tablespoons olive oil, lemon juice, and the remaining garlic in a small bowl. Season to taste with salt and pepper.

Punch down the dough. On a floured surface, divide the dough into 2 pieces and form into round balls. Roll 1 piece into a 9-inch (23-cm) circle, $^1/_4$-inch (0.6-cm) thick. Transfer it to a well-floured pizza peel or paddle. Brush the dough to within $^1/_2$ inch (1.25 cm) of the edge with the garlic-infused oil. Sprinkle the cheese mixture over the dough. Slide the pizza onto the pizza stone and bake until golden and crisp, 8 to 10 minutes. Toss the arugula with the vinaigrette and season with salt and pepper. Spread on top of pizza. Shave Parmigiano onto the top and serve immediately.

Make a second pizza with the remaining ingredients.

MAKES 2 PIZZAS, 9 INCHES (23CM) IN DIAMETER

Pizza with Salad on Top?

TOPPING PIZZAS WITH FRESH SALADS is now my favorite way to serve pizza. The idea is to bake the pizza with a basic combination of 1½ ounces mozzarella and 1½ ounces fontina. Sometimes, a few other ingredients are baked onto the top of the pizza, such as onions or peppers. When you take the pizza from the oven, top it with a few fresh ingredients. Sometimes it is a salad, sometimes it's a drizzle of a sauce like aioli. Here are a few other ideas.

* * *

1. Tapenade baked on the pizza, with a parsley and shaved Parmigiano salad on top
2. Tapenade baked on the pizza, with a salami and parsley salad on top
3. Colored bell peppers baked on the pizza, with a cherry tomato and basil salad on top
4. Colored bell peppers and jalapeños baked on the pizza, with a cherry tomato, cilantro, and lime salad on top
5. A few red onion slices baked on the pizza, with smoked salmon, caviar, chervil, and a drizzle of crème fraîche on top
6. Brandade (salt cod, potato, and garlic puree) baked on the pizza, with arugula on top
7. Tiny raw shrimp added halfway through the cooking, with a drizzle of aioli on top
8. A touch of tomato baked on the pizza, with arugula and prosciutto on top
9. A few red onion slices baked on the pizza, with an arugula, mint, cilantro, basil, and parsley salad dressed with lemon, garlic, and olive oil on top
10. Cheeses baked on the pizza, with a shaved fennel and parsley salad dressed with lemon, garlic, and olive oil on top

Two Dozen Pizza Ideas

ONCE YOU HAVE A FEW GUIDELINES FOR PIZZA-making, you will realize not only how easy they are to make, but that the possibilities are endless.

After you have rolled out your pizza dough, brush the top to within ½ inch of the edge with olive oil. This seals the crust so it doesn't get soggy. In most cases, the cheese is added next; that is, unless you are using tomato sauce. If tomato sauce is part of the pizza, it should be well reduced, to the consistency of tomato paste. Spread a couple of tablespoons of tomato sauce onto the top of the pizza, using the back of the spoon. For each 9-inch pizza, use a combination of 1½ ounces of coarsely grated mozzarella and 1½ ounces of coarsely grated fontina cheese sprinkled over the top.

A pizza cooks very quickly, in about 8 to 10 minutes, so remember, if the toppings take longer to cook—like sausage, eggplant, and wild mushrooms—cook them prior to baking the pizza dough.

* * *

1. Sausage, colored bell peppers, and cheeses
2. Wilted greens, olives, Parmigiano, and other cheeses
3. Peppers, capers, olives, and cheeses
4. Roasted onions, gorgonzola, and sage
5. Caramelized onions, goat cheese, thyme, and oregano
6. Roasted onions, olives, and anchovies
7. Stewed leeks, gorgonzola, and toasted walnuts
8. Stewed leeks, goat cheese, and toasted pine nuts
9. Buffalo or cow's milk mozzarella, basil, and tomato sauce
10. Wilted greens, pine nuts, capers, and raisins
11. Sun-dried tomato puree, roasted or grilled eggplant, and Parmigiano
12. Sun-dried tomato puree and olives
13. Tomato sauce with lots of garlic and roasted or grilled eggplant
14. Caramelized onions, olives, and anchovies
15. Stewed artichoke hearts with slivered garlic and pancetta
16. Roasted or grilled eggplant and pesto
17. Sautéed wild mushrooms, thyme, oregano, and sage
18. Roasted or grilled eggplant and basil
19. Stewed leeks, pancetta, and goat cheese
20. Sautéed slices of butternut squash, bacon, and sage
21. Oven-roasted tomatoes, slivered garlic, and truffle oil
22. Lamb sausage, oven-roasted tomatoes, roasted or grilled eggplant, and mint
23. Colored bell peppers, sausage, and cherry tomatoes
24. Sausage, toasted pine nuts, and roasted or grilled eggplant

Pizza with Asparagus, Prosciutto, and Truffle Oil

1 RECIPE PIZZA DOUGH (SEE PAGE 107)

1 GARLIC CLOVE, MINCED

2 TABLESPOONS EXTRA-VIRGIN OLIVE OIL

8 TO 10 ASPARAGUS SPEARS, ENDS TRIMMED, CUT INTO $1/2$-INCH (1.25-CM) PIECES ON THE DIAGONAL, ABOUT 6 OUNCES (180G)

$3/4$ CUP (3 OZ/90G) COARSELY GRATED MOZZARELLA CHEESE

$3/4$ CUP (3 OZ/90G) COARSELY GRATED FONTINA CHEESE

SALT

6 PAPER-THIN SLICES PROSCIUTTO, CUT INTO 1-INCH (2.5-CM) STRIPS

2 TABLESPOONS TRUFFLE OIL

Make the pizza dough and let rise.

Thirty minutes before baking, place a pizza stone or unglazed quarry tiles on the bottom shelf of the oven and set the oven temperature to 500°F (260°C).

Combine the garlic and olive oil and let stand for 30 minutes. In a bowl, combine the fontina and mozzarella and set aside.

Bring a saucepan of salted water to a boil. Add the asparagus and cook until just tender, 3 to 4 minutes. Drain and cool.

Punch down the dough. On a floured surface, divide the dough into 2 pieces and form into round balls. Roll 1 piece into a 9-inch (23-cm) circle, $1/4$-inch (0.6-cm) thick. Transfer it to a well-floured pizza peel or paddle. Brush the dough to within $1/2$ inch (1.25 cm) of the edge with the garlic-infused oil. Sprinkle the cheese mixture over the dough. Top with half of the asparagus, distributing evenly. Sprinkle with salt. Slide the pizza onto the pizza stone and bake until golden and crisp, 8 to 12 minutes. Top with half of the prosciutto, distributing evenly. Drizzle with half of the truffle oil and serve immediately.

Make a second pizza with the remaining ingredients.

MAKES 2 PIZZAS, 9 INCHES (23CM) IN DIAMETER

Asparagus, truffles, and prosciutto—the combination is delicate and delicious. If price is no object and truffles are in season, try shaving a few paper-thin slices of truffle, black or white, onto the top of the pizza just before serving. The truffles will add a bit of color and a blast of flavor.

Pizza with Cherry Tomato and Basil Salad

1 recipe Pizza Dough (see below)
1½ cups (6 oz/180g) coarsely grated mozzarella cheese
3 tablespoons (1½ fl oz/45ml) extra-virgin olive oil
3 tablespoons (1½ fl oz/45ml) balsamic vinegar
1 garlic clove, minced
Salt and freshly ground black pepper
6 ounces (180g) yellow cherry tomatoes, cut in half
6 ounces (180g) red cherry tomatoes, cut in half
1½ cups (6 oz/180g) coarsely grated mozzarella cheese
½ cup(1 oz/30g) loosely packed fresh basil leaves, cut into thin strips

Make the pizza dough and let rise.

Thirty minutes before baking, place a pizza stone or unglazed quarry tiles on the bottom shelf of the oven and set the oven temperature to 500°F (260°C).

On a floured surface, divide the dough into 2 pieces and form into round balls. Roll 1 piece into a 9-inch (23-cm) circle, ¼-inch (0.6cm) thick. Transfer to a well-floured pizza peel or paddle. Top with half of the cheese, distributing evenly. Transfer the pizza from the peel directly onto the heated stone in the oven. Bake until golden and crisp, 8 to 12 minutes.

In the meantime, whisk together the oil, vinegar, and garlic in a bowl. Season with salt and pepper. Add the cherry tomatoes and toss together.

When the pizza is done, place on a platter. Top with half of the tomatoes, vinaigrette, and basil. Serve immediately. Make a second pizza with the remaining ingredients.

Makes 2 pizzas, 9 inches (23cm) in diameter

When I have pizza, I have to accompany it with salad. So I call this my "everything-in-one" pizza, because I top crisp hot pizza fresh from the oven with a fresh salad. The vinaigrette drizzles onto the bread, combines with the melted cheese and crunchy crust. Then you taste the sweet cherry tomatoes and fresh basil. The combination can't be beat.

Pizza Dough

2 teaspoons active dry yeast
¾ cup plus 2 tablespoons lukewarm water (110°F/43°C)
2 cups unbleached bread flour
2 tablespoons olive oil
½ teaspoon salt

In a bowl, combine the yeast, ¼ cup warm water, and ¼ cup flour. Let it stand for 30 minutes. Add the remaining 1¾ cup flour, ½ cup plus 2 tablespoons warm water, olive oil, and salt. Mix the dough thoroughly and turn out onto a floured surface. Knead until smooth, elastic, and a bit tacky to the touch, 7 to 8 minutes. Place in an oiled bowl and turn to cover with oil. Cover with plastic wrap and let rise in a warm place (about 75°F/24°C) until it doubles in volume, 1 to 1½ hours. Or, let the dough rise in the refrigerator overnight. The next day, let it come to room temperature and proceed with the recipe.

Pizza with Smoked Trout and Caviar

Sometimes I call this celebration pizza because I always seem to serve this one with champagne for some occasion or another. In place of smoked trout, try substituting about 4 ounces (120g) of thinly sliced smoked salmon. And of course, as is always the case, buy the best caviar you feel you can afford that day.

1 RECIPE PIZZA DOUGH (SEE PAGE 107)
2 GARLIC CLOVES, MINCED
2 TABLESPOONS (1 FL OZ/30ML) EXTRA-VIRGIN OLIVE OIL
3/4 CUP (3 OZ/90G) COARSELY GRATED FONTINA CHEESE
3/4 CUP (3 OZ/90G) COARSELY GRATED MOZZARELLA CHEESE
1/2 SMALL RED ONION, VERY THINLY SLICED
6 OUNCES (180G) FLAKED SMOKED TROUT
1/3 CUP (2 1/2 FL OZ/75ML) CRÈME FRAÎCHE
SALT AND FRESHLY GROUND BLACK PEPPER
2 TABLESPOONS MINCED GREEN ONIONS OR CHIVES
1 OUNCE (30G) CAVIAR, BELUGA, SEVRUGA, OSETRA, OR
   AMERICAN STURGEON

Make the pizza dough and let rise.

Thirty minutes before baking, place a pizza stone or unglazed quarry tiles on the bottom shelf of the oven and set the oven temperature to 500°F (260°C).

Combine the garlic and olive oil and let the flavor of the garlic permeate the oil for 30 minutes. Combine the fontina and mozzarella. Reserve.

On a floured surface, divide the dough into 2 pieces and form into round balls. Roll 1 piece of dough into a 9-inch (23-cm) circle. Transfer to a well-floured pizza peel or paddle. Lightly brush the dough to within 1/2 inch (1.25 cm) of the edge with the garlic oil. Sprinkle half of the cheese over the oil, leaving 1/2 inch (1.25 cm) around the edge. Spread half of the onions on top of the cheese. Transfer the pizza from the peel directly onto the heated stone and bake until golden and crisp, 8 to 12 minutes. Remove from the oven.

Distribute the trout evenly over the top of the pizza. Season the crème fraîche with salt and pepper and add 1 or 2 tablespoons water to make an almost pourable consistency. Drizzle the crème fraîche lightly onto the top of the pizza. Garnish with green onions and caviar and serve immediately.

Make a second pizza with the remaining ingredients.

MAKES 2 PIZZAS, 9 INCHES (23CM) IN DIAMETER

Pizza with Gorgonzola and Tomatoes

1 RECIPE PIZZA DOUGH (SEE PAGE 107)
2 GARLIC CLOVES, MINCED
3 TABLESPOONS (1$^1/_2$ FL OZ/45 ML) EXTRA-VIRGIN OLIVE OIL
$^1/_2$ CUP (2 OZ/60G) COARSELY GRATED FONTINA CHEESE
$^1/_2$ CUP (2 OZ/60G) COARSELY GRATED MOZZARELLA CHEESE
4 OUNCES GORGONZOLA CHEESE
12 PLUM TOMATOES, PEELED, SEEDED, AND CHOPPED
SALT AND FRESHLY GROUND BLACK PEPPER

Make the pizza dough and let rise.

Thirty minutes before baking, place a pizza stone or unglazed quarry tiles on the bottom shelf of the oven and set the oven temperature to 500°F (260°C).

In a small bowl, combine the garlic and 2 tablespoons of the olive oil and let stand for 30 minutes. In another bowl, combine the fontina, mozzarella, and Gorgonzola cheeses and reserve.

In a saucepan over high heat, heat the remaining 1 tablespoon olive oil. Add the tomatoes and bring to a boil. Reduce the heat to low and simmer until the tomatoes are very dry and $^1/_2$ cup (4 fl oz/125 ml) remains, 15 to 20 minutes. Season to taste with salt and pepper. Let cool.

Punch down the dough. On a floured surface, divide the dough into 2 pieces and form into round balls. Roll 1 piece into a 9-inch circle, $^1/_4$-inch (0.6cm) thick. Transfer it to a well-floured pizza peel or paddle. Brush the dough to within $^1/_2$ inch (1.25 cm) of the edge with the garlic-infused oil. Spread half of the tomato sauce on top of the oil to within $^1/_2$ inch (1.25 cm) of the edge. Sprinkle with half of the cheese. Slide the pizza onto the pizza stone and bake until golden and crisp, 8 to 12 minutes. Remove from the oven and serve immediately.

Make a second pizza with the remaining ingredients.

MAKES 2 PIZZAS, 9 INCHES (23CM) IN DIAMETER

I think tomatoes and gorgonzola are a match made in heaven. A few years ago, I visited a little hole-in-the-wall pizza joint I had heard was the absolute "best of the best" pizza in San Francisco. When I got there, I just couldn't decide on which pizza I wanted. But when this one arrived at my table, the Gorgonzola melting with the tomatoes, I knew I had made the right choice.

You Don't Need a Pizza Oven?

IT IS SO EASY TO MAKE GOOD PIZZAS AT HOME in your own oven. There are only a few things to remember.

First, you need an oven that reaches at least 500°F. Ideally you want your oven between 500°F and 700°F (300°C and 370°C), so the hotter your oven the better.

Next, you need a pizza stone or unglazed quarry tiles, set on the bottom shelf of your oven. If you are using quarry tiles, push them together so you have enough surface to set your pizza on top. Remember, and this is very important, before you place your pizza in the oven, you need to heat the pizza stone or quarry tiles to your oven's hottest temperature for at least thirty minutes. Don't even think about putting your pizza in the oven onto a cold stone. It would defeat the whole purpose.

You also need a pizza peel or paddle, preferably made of wood. Once you make the dough, you will want to place it on the well-floured peel. And when the stone is hot, you will transfer the pizza from the peel to the stone, holding the peel at a 20° angle, touching the tip of the peel to the stone as you slide the pizza directly off the peel onto the stone. Bake the pizza until it is golden and crisp.

See, there really is nothing to it!

Calzone Dough

2 TEASPOONS ACTIVE DRY YEAST
1 CUP (8 FL OZ/240ML) LUKEWARM WATER (110°F/43°C)
3 CUPS (12$^1/_2$ OZ/375G) UNBLEACHED BREAD FLOUR
SALT
3 TABLESPOONS (1$^1/_2$ FL OZ/45ML) EXTRA-VIRGIN OLIVE OIL

Combine the yeast, $^1/_2$ cup (4 fl oz/125 ml) lukewarm water, and $^1/_2$ cup (2 oz/60g) flour in a large bowl. Let it sit until it bubbles up, about 30 minutes. Add the remaining 2$^1/_2$ cups (10$^1/_2$ oz/315g) flour, $^3/_4$ teaspoon salt, olive oil, and $^1/_2$ cup (4 fl oz/120ml) lukewarm water. Mix the dough thoroughly. Turn out onto a floured surface and knead until smooth, elastic, and a bit tacky to the touch, 7 to 8 minutes. Place in an oiled bowl and turn to cover with oil. Cover with plastic wrap and let rise in a warm place (75°F/26°C) until doubled in volume, 1 to 1$^1/_2$ hours.

Alternately you can let this dough rise in the refrigerator overnight. The next day, bring the dough to room temperature and proceed.

Calzone with Oven-Dried Tomatoes and Roasted Peppers

1 CUP (3^1/$_2$ OZ/100G) OVEN-DRIED PLUM TOMATOES (SEE NOTE),
   THINLY SLICED

^{1}/$_4$ CUP (1^1/$_2$ OZ/45G) PITTED, COARSELY CHOPPED NIÇOISE OR
   KALAMATA OLIVES

2 TABLESPOONS CAPERS

1 RED BELL PEPPER, ROASTED AND CUT INTO STRIPS (SEE PAGE 27)

^{1}/$_2$ CUP (2 OZ/60G) GRATED FONTINA CHEESE

^{1}/$_2$ CUP (2 OZ/60G) GRATED MOZZARELLA CHEESE

1 CUP (5 OZ/150G) CRUMBLED GOAT CHEESE

2 TABLESPOONS CHOPPED FRESH BASIL

1 TABLESPOON CHOPPED FRESH MINT

2 TEASPOONS CHOPPED FRESH OREGANO

1 RECIPE CALZONE DOUGH (SEE PAGE 110)

I love dishes like calzone that look as though they are complicated to make but instead are really easy. The finished results are quite impressive. The best part is delivering the dish to the table and hearing the guests say their "oohs and ahs." Let's face it, why do we cook?

Sometimes instead of making two large calzone, I prefer to make four individual ones and serve each guest his or her own. With a green salad, it makes a perfect main course.

Thirty minutes before baking, place a pizza stone or unglazed quarry tiles on the bottom shelf of the oven and set the oven temperature to 500°F (260°C).

In a bowl, combine the tomatoes, olives, capers, red bell pepper, fontina, mozzarella, goat cheese, basil, mint, and oregano.

On a floured surface, divide the dough into 2 pieces and form into round balls. Roll 1 piece of the dough into a 12-inch (30-cm) circle, approximately ^{1}/$_4$-inch (0.6-cm) thick and place it on a well-floured pizza peel or paddle. Spread half of the tomato and cheese mixture on half of the dough, leaving a 1^1/$_2$-inch (4-cm) border around the edge. With a pastry brush, moisten the bottom edges of the dough lightly with water and fold the dough over the filling, matching the edges and pressing together well to seal completely. Roll the edges of the dough inward and press to make a tight seal. Slide the calzone onto the pizza stone and bake until golden and crisp, 10 to 12 minutes. Remove from the oven and place on a wooden cutting board. Let rest for 10 minutes before serving. Repeat with the remaining dough.

MAKES 2 LARGE OR 4 INDIVIDUAL-SIZE CALZONE AND SERVES 4

NOTE: TO MAKE OVEN-DRIED TOMATOES, PLACE 3 POUNDS (1.35KG) PLUM TOMATOES, CORED AND CUT IN HALF LENGTHWISE, ON A BAKING SHEET, CUT SIDE UP, AND SPRINKLE WITH SALT. LET SIT FOR 1 HOUR. BAKE IN A 250°F (120°C) OVEN FOR 5 TO 6 HOURS, UNTIL NEARLY DRY.

Harvest Flatbread with Grapes and Walnuts

One autumn in Napa there was a bumper crop of grapes and everywhere you went grapes were being picked with the speed of lightning. I went into a little cantinetta in St. Helena, where they were making this flatbread topped with all different kinds of fresh grapes—chardonnay, pinot noir, and tiny green champagne grapes. The top was drizzled with local olive oil. I grabbed a flatbread hot from the oven and a bottle of wine and made a mad dash for a picnic.

$^1/_4$ CUP (2 FL OZ/60ML) EXTRA-VIRGIN OLIVE OIL

3 SPRIGS OF ROSEMARY

1 TABLESPOON ACTIVE DRY YEAST

2 CUPS (8 OZ/250G) UNBLEACHED BREAD FLOUR

$^3/_4$ CUP (6 FL OZ/185ML) LUKEWARM WATER (110°F/43°C)

1 TABLESPOON ANISE SEED, COARSELY GROUND

SALT

2 TABLESPOONS SUGAR

$^1/_2$ CUP ($2^1/_2$ OZ/75G) WALNUTS, TOASTED (SEE PAGE 78) AND
    VERY COARSELY CHOPPED

$1^1/_2$ CUPS (9 OZ/270G) GRAPES, ANY VARIETY

COARSE SALT

With the spine of a chef's knife, tap the rosemary sprigs gently to bruise the stems slightly. Heat the olive oil and rosemary over medium heat until it sizzles, about 2 minutes. Remove from the heat and let cool. Remove the rosemary sprigs.

In a small bowl, stir together the yeast, $^1/_4$ cup (1 oz/30g) of the flour, and $^1/_4$ cup (2 fl oz/60ml) warm water. Let stand until the mixture bubbles, 30 minutes. Add the anise seeds, $^1/_2$ teaspoon salt, the sugar, remaining $1^3/_4$ cups (7 oz/220g) flour, remaining $^1/_2$ cup (4 fl oz/125 ml) warm water, walnuts, and rosemary oil. Mix the ingredients together thoroughly with a wooden spoon. Turn the mixture out onto a floured board and knead until the dough is smooth and elastic, 7 to 8 minutes. Place the dough in a well-oiled bowl and turn it over to oil the top. Cover with plastic wrap and let rise in a warm place (75°F/26°C) until doubled in volume, 1 to 1 $^1/_2$ hours.

Preheat the oven to 450°F (230°C). Place a pizza stone on the bottom shelf of the oven for at least 30 minutes before baking the flatbread.

After the dough has doubled in volume, punch it down to deflate the bubbles. On a heavily floured surface, roll the dough to an 8- x 10-inch (20- x 25-cm) oval, $^1/_2$-inch (1.25-cm) thick. Transfer to a well-floured pizza peel. With your fingertips, make slight indentations in the dough. Press the grapes into the top and sprinkle with 1 teaspoon coarse salt. Bake on the pizza stone until golden and crisp, 12 to 15 minutes.

Serve hot, warm, or at room temperature.

SERVES 6

Streams, Riv

STREAMS,

My father is a quiet man. Getting a rise out of him has never been easy. When I was a kid, I'd do anything to make him pay attention to me.

In our family of cooks and food lovers, everyone had their signature dish, and my father's specialty was oysters. He loved them in any shape or form, cooked or raw, in soups, stews, or omelets. He'd grab a wooden-handled oyster knife, wrap a towel around his hand, and in a flash, open a dozen oysters, popping off the top shell and slipping the knife under the meat to detach it. That was his favorite way to eat them: right from the shell, topped with a little freshly grated horseradish.

I remember watching him and thinking how happy he looked, as his eyes rolled in an expression of exaggerated bliss. And so one day, when I was around six, I decided it was time to give this oyster thing a try. I remember the shock of feeling that first icy-cold oyster slide down my throat. But when I looked up and saw my dad grinning from ear to ear, I picked up one oyster after another and slurped fearlessly away. He was impressed and more than a little proud to see such a young kid take on his favorite food—admittedly an acquired taste.

Well, I acquired the taste, all right, and today, oysters are one of my most beloved indulgences. The Northern Pacific coast offers a huge variety of fish and shellfish, including salmon, squid, and our world famous Dungeness crabs. But I'd trade them all for a few really good oysters. So in the name of research, I headed up the coast to Tomales Bay, north of San Francisco in Marin County, to spend a day with the boys at the Hog Island Oyster Company.

After about an hour of winding roads and glorious scenery, I rounded a bend and came upon the loveliest of coves and a signpost indicating that I had arrived in the town of Marshall, population 35. The locals like to call this place "the Malibu of Northern California," but it's really not much more than the office of the Hog Island Oyster Company and the ramshackle shell of an abandoned oyster restaurant, hugging the water's edge.

Oysters are native to the clean waters of Tomales Bay. They were a famous delicacy of the gold-rush era

ers, the Sea

RIV'ERS, THE SEA

Delicious fresh seafood is a specialty along the Northern California coast.
Opposite: Streams and rivers provide a shelter for trout and spawning salmon.

and they've been a fixture of San Francisco high life ever since. But it wasn't until the 1980s that a real renaissance of oyster and mussel farming began on the bay, and Hog Island was the first company on the scene.

Terry Sawyer, who is in charge of technical operations, greeted me with a smile and a pair of chest-high waders. It was low tide, and we headed out to the oyster beds in the middle of the bay to join the Hog Island crew. Our first stop was the nursery, where millions of baby oysters spend their infancy. It's not a bad childhood; the tiny oysters, not much more than a quarter of an inch long, are gently rocked in floating cradles by the flow of the tides.

Once the baby oysters have tripled in size, it's time to transfer them to the grow-out beds. It occurred to me that maybe the reason they're called oyster beds is that these contraptions look just like floating box springs. In the business, they're known as "racks and bags," and it's here that the oysters mature, two hundred to the bag, a thousand in each rack, their tranquillity interrupted only by the oystermen's occasional banging, which keeps the oysters from growing together in clumps.

Once they're mature, they're brought to shore and sorted by size. The smallest—the best for eating raw—go to the restaurant trade, while the larger ones are sold for cooking and barbecuing.

At Hog Island, the harvest continues year-round, weather permitting. The best oysters for cooking and barbecuing are harvested in the summer, while winter is generally the season for the best oysters on the half shell. Hog Island raises several varieties: small, buttery Kumamotos; round, flat French Belons; the prized Sweetwater; and my favorite, the briny Atlantic Blue Point.

After a long day of wading through chilly water, I'd come to understand how these delicate bivalves are lovingly raised from infancy to maturity. Now it was time to eat them!

At a huge sorting table on the dock, I joined the crew and helped shuck our lunch. Shucking oysters is like riding a bike. Once you do it a few thousand times—as I did when I worked at Chez Panisse—you never forget how. The trick is to slip the knife into the hinge end, pop the top open and run the knife along the edge until the top comes off. Then you cut the tendon that holds the oyster to the shell. As a finishing touch, you can flip the oyster in the shell to show its smooth underside.

We started with a sampling of raw oysters on the half-shell, floating in their salty liquor—some of the cleanest and sweetest I've ever tasted. Then we shared a few dozen barbecued oysters, the local specialty, cooked in their shells over coals and topped with a spicy, homemade tomato-horseradish sauce. We washed it all down with a dry Sauvignon Blanc, staring out at the sunset and the gently rippling water. These people live right.

Heading back to the city, my car weighted down with a huge crate of oysters, I couldn't help thinking how big my father's smile would be if he could only take a look in my trunk.

Oyster beds at Hog Island Oyster Company in Marshall, California.

Linguine with Spicy-Hot Crab and Tomatoes

2 Dungeness or blue crabs, 1 to 1$^1/_2$ pounds (450 to 675g) each, cooked
$^1/_4$ cup (2 fl oz/60ml) extra-virgin olive oil
5 garlic cloves, crushed
1$^1/_2$ cups (12 fl oz/360ml) dry red wine, such as Cabernet Sauvignon
5 cups (40 oz/1.4kg) peeled, seeded, and chopped tomatoes, fresh or canned
2 cups (16 fl oz/900ml) bottled clam juice or fish stock
3 tablespoons (1$^1/_2$ fl oz/45ml) red wine vinegar
12 basil leaves, torn into small pieces
1 teaspoon chopped fresh oregano or marjoram
1$^1/_4$ teaspoons crushed red pepper flakes
Salt
1 pound (450g) dry linguine
20 basil leaves, cut into thin strips, as a garnish

Clean and crack the crab, or have your fishmonger do it. Cut the claws and bodies into several pieces.

In a saucepan, heat the olive oil over medium-low heat. Add the garlic and cook until soft, but not golden, about 1 minute. Remove the garlic and discard. Add the wine, increase the heat to high, and simmer until it has reduced by three-quarters, 5 to 7 minutes. Using a food mill, puree the tomatoes directly into the pan. Add the fish stock, vinegar, basil, oregano, red pepper flakes, and salt to taste. As soon as the mixture comes to a boil, reduce the heat to medium-low, and simmer until slightly thickened, 8 to 10 minutes. Add the crab and continue to cook for 5 minutes. Taste and season with salt.

Bring a large pot of salted water to a boil. Add the pasta and cook until al dente, 5 to 8 minutes. Drain and toss with the crab and tomato sauce. Serve immediately, garnished with basil.

Serves 6

*D*ungeness crab is one of the greatest gifts from the sea, as sweet as it can be. James Beard, American cook extraordinaire, always said it was his favorite food in the world. Combine it with sweet tomatoes, basil, and just the right amount of crushed red pepper flakes to leave you with a bite of hot on the back of your throat.

Roasted Corn and Crab Chowder

6 MEDIUM EARS OF FRESH CORN IN THEIR HUSKS

2 DUNGENESS OR BLUE CRABS, 1 TO 1½ POUNDS (450 TO 700G) EACH,
     COOKED

2 TABLESPOONS UNSALTED BUTTER

1 SMALL YELLOW ONION, CHOPPED

4 FRESH THYME SPRIGS

3 BAY LEAVES

1½ CUPS (12 FL OZ/360ML) DRY WHITE WINE, SUCH AS SAUVIGNON BLANC

3 CUPS (24 FL OZ/725ML) BOTTLED CLAM JUICE OR FISH STOCK

¾ POUND (350G) POTATOES, PEELED AND CUT INTO
     ½-INCH (1.25-CM) DICE

½ CUP (4 FL OZ/120ML) HEAVY CREAM

SALT AND FRESHLY GROUND BLACK PEPPER

1 TABLESPOON FINELY SNIPPED CHIVES

It's too bad summer is so short—and with it the season for corn! There is nothing like the slightly smoky flavor of corn roasted on a grill. If by chance you have some leftover ears, save them for this soup. The sweetness of crab combined with fresh butter-and-sugar corn makes a delicious chowder. The only thing missing is a bottle of chilled Chardonnay. You can make the soup a couple of days ahead, store in the refrigerator, and heat just before serving.

Heat a charcoal grill. Grill the corn 4 inches from the coals, turning occasionally, until the corn husks are black and the corn kernels are light golden when the husk is pulled back, 6 to 10 minutes. Remove the husks and silk and discard. Cut the kernels from the cob and set aside.

Clean and crack the crab, or have your fishmonger do it, and remove the meat from the body and legs. Reserve in a bowl. Remove the meat from the claws and slice. Add to the bowl with the other crab meat. Using heavy kitchen shears, cut the shells into small pieces and set aside.

In a soup pot over low heat, melt the butter. Add the onions and cook, stirring occasionally, until soft, 10 minutes. Add the crab shells, thyme, bay leaves, wine, clam juice, and 1½ cups (12 fl oz/350ml) water. Bring to a boil, reduce the heat to low, cover, and simmer 20 minutes. Strain and discard the shells.

Reserve 1 cup (6 oz/180g) corn for a garnish. Add the remaining corn to the crab broth and simmer until reduced by one quarter, about 15 minutes. In batches, puree the soup in a blender on high speed, 3 minutes per batch, until very smooth. Strain through a fine mesh strainer lined with cheesecloth into a clean soup pan.

Bring a large saucepan three-quarters full of salted water to a boil. Add the potatoes and cook until tender, about 10 minutes. Drain and reserve.

Add the cream, reserved crab meat, reserved corn, and the potatoes. Season to taste with salt and pepper. Heat over medium high heat just until hot, 3 to 4 minutes. Serve immediately, garnished with chives.

SERVES 6

Shellfish Cakes with Lime Tartar Sauce

1¼ CUPS (10 FL OZ/300ML) PREPARED OR HOMEMADE MAYONNAISE
   (SEE PAGE 52)
1 TEASPOON DIJON MUSTARD
1 TEASPOON GRATED LIME ZEST
1 TABLESPOON LIME JUICE
¼ CUP (1½ OZ/45G) MINCED CORNICHONS (GHERKINS)
SALT AND FRESHLY GROUND BLACK PEPPER
2 TABLESPOONS UNSALTED BUTTER
1 BUNCH OF GREEN ONIONS, WHITE AND GREEN, THINLY SLICED
¾ CUP (3½ OZ/100G) CHOPPED CELERY
1 CUP (3 OZ/90G) CRUSHED SALTINES
1 TABLESPOON DRY MUSTARD
1 TEASPOON HOT PEPPER SAUCE, SUCH AS TABASCO
2 TEASPOONS WORCESTERSHIRE SAUCE
2 EGGS, WELL BEATEN
3 TABLESPOONS (¼ OZ/8G) FINELY CHOPPED FLAT-LEAF PARSLEY
6 OUNCES (180G) COOKED CRAB MEAT
6 OUNCES (180G) COOKED SHRIMP, PEELED AND CHOPPED
6 OUNCES (180G) COOKED SCALLOPS, CHOPPED
2 CUPS FRESH BREAD CRUMBS
¼ CUP (2 FL OZ/60ML) VEGETABLE OIL OR MELTED BUTTER

*W*hy is it that whenever any-one sees crab cakes, shrimp cakes, or shellfish cakes on a menu, they feel they must order them? Try making them at home. They are so simple. I have been using this recipe for years, serving them with all kinds of sauces.

For the tartar sauce, combine 1 cup (8 fl oz/240ml) of the mayonnaise, the mustard, lime zest, lime juice, and cornichons in a bowl and mix well. Season to taste with salt and pepper.

Melt the butter in a large skillet and cook the green onions and celery slowly in a covered pan, stirring occasionally, until they are soft, about 12 minutes. Drain and cool. Add the saltines, mustard, hot pepper sauce, Worcestershire, eggs, remaining ¼ cup (2 fl oz/60ml) mayonnaise, parsley, crab meat, shrimp, scallops, and salt and pepper. Mix well. If the mixture is wet, add enough bread crumbs to absorb the moisture so they hold their shape. Shape the batter into 2½-inch (6-cm) cakes. Dredge them lightly in the bread crumbs.

Heat 2 tablespoons oil in a skillet over medium heat. Sauté the shellfish cakes in a single layer, 3 minutes per side, until golden brown. Drain on paper towels. Repeat with the remaining oil and crab cakes. Serve immediately with the Lime Tartar Sauce.

SERVES 6

Shellfish Stew with Orzo

3 CUPS (24 FL OZ/725ML) BOTTLED CLAM JUICE OR FISH STOCK

1 POUND (450G) CLAMS

1 POUND (450G) MUSSELS

$1/2$ POUND (240G) SCALLOPS

$1/2$ POUND (240G) MEDIUM SHRIMP, PEELED AND DEVEINED

3 TABLESPOONS ($1^{1}/_{2}$ FL OZ/45ML) EXTRA-VIRGIN OLIVE OIL

1 SMALL YELLOW ONION, MINCED

3 GARLIC CLOVES, MINCED

1 SMALL PINCH OF CRUSHED RED PEPPER FLAKES

1 CUP (8 FL OZ/240ML) DRY WHITE WINE, SUCH AS SAUVIGNON BLANC

2 BAY LEAVES

$1^{1}/_{2}$ CUPS (12 OZ/350G) PEELED, SEEDED, AND CHOPPED TOMATOES,
    FRESH OR CANNED

1 TEASPOON RED WINE VINEGAR

SALT AND FRESHLY GROUND BLACK PEPPER

1 CUP (5 OZ/150G) ORZO

3 TABLESPOONS ($1/4$ OZ/8G) CHOPPED FRESH FLAT-LEAF PARSLEY

LARGE PINCH OF SAFFRON THREADS

Bring the clam juice to a boil in a large soup pot over medium high heat. Add the clams, cover, and cook until the clams open, 3 to 4 minutes. As the clams open, remove them from the pan with tongs and place them in a large bowl. Discard any that have not opened. Remove the shells from half of the clams. Repeat with the mussels, cooking for 2 to 3 minutes. Remove half the shells from the mussels and add them to the clams. Reserve the broth. Remove the muscle from the side of each scallop. Add the raw scallops and shrimp to the cooked shellfish. Reserve.

Heat the olive oil in the soup pot. Add the onions and sauté until soft, about 7 minutes. Add the garlic and crushed red pepper and sauté for 1 minute. Turn the heat to high and immediately add the wine. Reduce by one-half, about 2 minutes. Add $1^{1}/_{2}$ cups (12 fl oz/350ml) water, the bay leaves, tomatoes, vinegar, and reserved broth, and bring to a boil. Reduce the heat to low, add the orzo, cover, and simmer for 2 minutes. Add the parsley, saffron, and shellfish to the soup pot and simmer for 2 minutes. Turn off the heat and let sit for 3 minutes. Season to taste with salt and pepper.

Ladle the soup into bowls, distributing the shellfish evenly, and serve immediately.

SERVES 6

Off the coast of northern California, we have some excellent shellfish, which was the inspiration for this stew. If you are landlocked, the trick here is a simple one—start with the freshest shellfish. My first choice would be to suggest you grab some fishing nets and rent a boat. But maybe a bit more practical is to buy the freshest shellfish available from your favorite fishmonger.

Seared Scallops
with Watercress and Lemon Relish

6 TABLESPOONS (3 FL OZ/90ML) EXTRA-VIRGIN OLIVE OIL

2 TEASPOONS GRATED LEMON ZEST

2 TABLESPOONS CHOPPED FRESH FLAT-LEAF PARSLEY

2 SHALLOTS, MINCED

2 TABLESPOONS LEMON JUICE

SALT AND FRESHLY GROUND BLACK PEPPER

1$\frac{1}{2}$ POUNDS (675G) SEA SCALLOPS

1 BUNCH OF WATERCRESS, STEMS REMOVED

LEMON WEDGES AS A GARNISH

In a small bowl, whisk together 4 tablespoons (2 fl oz/60ml) of the olive oil, the lemon zest, parsley, shallots, and lemon juice. Season to taste with salt and pepper.

Remove the muscle from the side of each scallop and discard. In a large skillet over medium high heat, warm the remaining 2 tablespoons olive oil. Add the scallops in a single layer. Do not overcrowd the pan. Cook the scallops until golden on 1 side, about 2 minutes. Turn the scallops, season with salt and pepper, and continue to cook until the scallops are golden and slightly firm to the touch, 2 to 3 minutes.

To serve, divide the scallops among 6 serving plates. Spoon the relish over the scallops, distributing evenly. Top with the watercress, garnish with lemon wedges, and serve immediately.

SERVES 6

I worked at Chez Panisse for years, and now, every time I go back, I say I am going to give up cooking! The food relies on a few simple principles: The ingredients are of the best quality, the fruits and vegetables full of flavor, and the fish is the freshest it can be. Instead of giving up, I usually just come home and reproduce the dishes with my own spin, which was exactly the inspiration for this dish.

Risotto with Lemon Shrimp

Making good risotto requires a bit of muscle. Making great risotto requires a bit of muscle and a little trick I learned in northern Italy. Begin tasting the rice after about 15 minutes. Just when it gets past the chalky stage, remove the pan from the heat, add a ladle of broth, a bit of butter, and the Parmigiano and let it sit, covered, for 5 minutes. Give it a stir and you have creamy risotto. Perfetto!

$1^1/_2$ POUNDS (24 OZ/675G) MEDIUM SHRIMP, PEELED, DEVEINED, AND
  SHELLS RESERVED
2 CUPS (16 FL OZ/475ML) BOTTLED CLAM JUICE
$1^1/_4$ CUP (10 FL OZ/275ML) DRY WHITE WINE, SUCH AS SAUVIGNON BLANC
4 TABLESPOONS (2 FL OZ/60ML) EXTRA-VIRGIN OLIVE OIL
1 MEDIUM ONION, CHOPPED
2 CUPS (10 OZ/300G) ARBORIO, VIALONE NANO, OR CARNAROLI RICE
3 TABLESPOONS ($1^1/_2$ FL OZ/45ML) LEMON JUICE
2 TABLESPOONS UNSALTED BUTTER
$^3/_4$ CUP (3 OZ/90G) GRATED PARMIGIANO REGGIANO CHEESE
$1^1/_2$ TEASPOONS GRATED LEMON ZEST
SALT AND FRESHLY GROUND BLACK PEPPER
FLAT-LEAF PARSLEY LEAVES, AS A GARNISH

Place the shrimp shells, clam juice, 3 cups (24 fl oz/720ml) water, and $^1/_2$ cup (4 fl oz/125 ml) of the wine in a saucepan. Bring to a boil over high heat. Reduce to low, cover, and simmer slowly for 15 minutes. Strain the shrimp stock and place in a saucepan on the back burner of the stove, adjusting the heat to maintain just below a simmer.

In a large heavy saucepan over medium-high heat, warm 2 tablespoons of the olive oil. Add the shrimp and cook until they curl slightly, about 2 minutes. Add $^1/_4$ cup (2 fl oz/60ml) of the wine and reduce by half. Remove the mixture from the pan and reserve.

Add the remaining 2 tablespoons olive oil to the pan. Add the onions and cook until soft, about 7 minutes. Add the rice and stir to coat the grains with oil, about 3 minutes. Add the remaining $^1/_2$ cup wine and $1^1/_2$ tablespoons lemon juice and cook, stirring, until the liquid evaporates, about 1 minute. Add about 1 cup of warm shrimp stock, stirring the rice constantly. When most of the liquid has been absorbed, add another ladleful of stock and continue to cook until the rice is just beyond the chalky stage, 18 to 22 minutes. If you run out of stock, use hot water.

Remove the pan from the heat, add the shrimp, a ladle of stock, the butter, half the Parmigiano, the lemon zest, and the remaining $1^1/_2$ tablespoons lemon juice. Season to taste with salt and pepper. Cover and let stand for 5 minutes. Remove the cover and stir. Place in serving bowls, sprinkle with the remaining Parmigiano, and serve immediately, garnished with parsley.

SERVES 6

Fried Oyster "Caesar"

18 FRESH OYSTERS, IN THE SHELL

$1/2$ CUP (2 OZ/60G) ALL-PURPOSE FLOUR

2 WHOLE EGGS

1 CUP ($3^{1}/_{2}$ OZ/100G) DRY BREAD CRUMBS

SALT AND FRESHLY GROUND BLACK PEPPER

OIL FOR DEEP FRYING (PEANUT, CORN, OR OLIVE OIL)

1 GARLIC CLOVE, MINCED

1 TEASPOON DIJON MUSTARD

$2^{1}/_{2}$ TABLESPOONS ($1^{1}/_{4}$ FL OZ/40ML) LEMON JUICE

2 ANCHOVY FILLETS, SOAKED IN COLD WATER FOR 10 MINUTES,
    PATTED DRY, AND MASHED

1 EGG YOLK

$1/3$ CUP (3 FL OZ/80ML) EXTRA-VIRGIN OLIVE OIL

4 SMALL HEARTS OF ROMAINE, LEAVES SEPARATED

$1/2$ CUP (2 OZ/60G) GRATED PARMIGIANO REGGIANO CHEESE

Shuck the oysters and reserve them separately from the oyster liquor. Discard the shells.

Place the flour in a bowl. Place the eggs in another bowl and whisk in 2 tablespoons water. Place the bread crumbs in a third bowl. Season the flour and bread crumbs with salt and pepper. Dredge the oysters in the flour first and tap off the excess. Next dip them in the egg mixture, and then in the bread crumbs. Reserve and set aside.

In a small saucepan, heat 1 inch (2.5cm) of oil to 375°F (190°C).

For the dressing, whisk together the reserved oyster liquor, the garlic, mustard, lemon juice, mashed anchovies, and egg yolk in a bowl until well blended. Add the olive oil in a slow, steady stream and whisk until smooth. Season to taste with salt and pepper.

Fry the oysters, a few at a time, until golden, about 1 minute. Remove with a slotted spoon and drain on paper towels.

Place the lettuce in a large bowl and toss with the dressing until the leaves are coated. Add half of the Parmigiano and toss again. Place on serving plates and top each plate with 3 oysters and sprinkle the top with the remaining Parmigiano. Serve immediately.

SERVES 6

Just North of San Francisco in the area of Tomales Bay, some of the best oysters in the world are raised. And when it's oyster season, there are plenty. I came up with this idea one day when I was driving back to the city with a full basket of fresh oysters. I have been making it ever since—regularly!

Warm Squid Salad
with Tangerine Oil and Olives

5 TANGERINES
$1/_4$ CUP (2 FL OZ/60ML) EXTRA-VIRGIN OLIVE OIL
$1^1/_4$ POUNDS (500G) SQUID
3 GARLIC CLOVES, MINCED
8 OUNCES (240G) SMALL CHERRY TOMATOES, RED AND YELLOW
3 TABLESPOONS ($1/_4$ OZ/8G) CHOPPED FRESH FLAT-LEAF PARSLEY
$3/_4$ CUP ($4^1/_2$ OZ/135G) IMPORTED BLACK OLIVES
SALT AND FRESHLY GROUND BLACK PEPPER
1 TABLESPOON LEMON JUICE

In the last few years, flavored oils have packed the grocery store shelves. There are some excellent ones, however. I have found them flavored with tangerines, but also made with oranges, limes, and lemons. If you prefer to purchase prepared citrus oil, do so by all means!

Remove the peel from the tangerines with a vegetable peeler. Warm the olive oil in a saucepan over medium heat. Add the tangerine peel and immediately remove the oil from the heat. Stir together. Let sit for 1 hour, then strain and reserve the peel. Thinly slice 2 tablespoons of the tangerine peel and reserve. Squeeze 1 tablespoon tangerine juice and reserve.

Separate the head and tentacles from the body of the squid. Cut the head from the tentacles and discard the head. Remove the clear quill bone from inside the body of each squid. With a knife, scrape away the skin, cleaning out the inside of the body at the same time. Cut the bodies into $1/_2$-inch (1.25-cm) rings. Wash the bodies and tentacles well until the water runs clear.

In a large skillet over high heat, warm the tangerine oil. Add the garlic and cook just until soft, a few seconds. Add the squid and cook, stirring, until the squid turn from opaque to white and the rings are slightly firm, 1 to $1^1/_2$ minutes. Remove the squid from the pan with a slotted spoon and reserve in a bowl. Increase the heat to high and reduce by half any liquid that has accumulated in the pan. Add the tomatoes and continue to cook for 30 seconds. Remove from the heat, add the parsley, olives, reserved tangerine juice, and lemon juice. Add the squid and toss together. Season to taste with salt and pepper. Place on a platter and serve immediately, garnished with the reserved tangerine peel.

SERVES 6

Charcoal-Grilled Oysters
with Sweet and Hot Red Peppers

$^1/_2$ CUP (4 FL OZ/120ML) RED WINE, SUCH AS CABERNET SAUVIGNON,
   MERLOT, OR ZINFANDEL
3 TABLESPOONS (1$^1/_2$ FL OZ/45ML) RED WINE VINEGAR
1 SHALLOT, MINCED
$^1/_2$ RED BELL PEPPER, ROASTED AND DICED (SEE PAGE 27)
PINCH OF CRUSHED RED PEPPER FLAKES
SALT AND FRESHLY GROUND BLACK PEPPER
ROCK SALT FOR SERVING
2 DOZEN FRESH OYSTERS, IN THE SHELL

Heat a charcoal grill and adjust the rack so it is 1 inch (2.5cm) above
the coals.

In a small bowl, whisk together the red wine, red wine vinegar, shallot,
red bell pepper, and red pepper flakes. Season to taste with salt and pepper.

In the meantime, spread 2 large ovenproof platters with about $^1/_2$ inch
(1.25cm) of rock salt. Place the oysters directly on the grill, curved side
down. When the shells just open slightly and begin bubbling, remove
the oysters from the fire, 2 to 4 minutes. Finish opening the oysters
with an oyster knife and discard the top shell. Place the oysters on the
rock salt in a single layer. Put a couple teaspoons of the sauce on each
oyster and serve immediately.

SERVES 6

There is something gratifying about watching the oyster shells pop open as they roast on the grill. This is a simple dish to make, but the flavors are all right there. Sweet, salt, sour, and smoky all in one bite—this is the way I love to eat. Serve these oysters on a bed of rock salt as a first course, with fresh rye bread slathered with sweet butter.

Grilled Swordfish Skewers with Olive "Caviar"

2 LEMONS

1/2 CUP (4 FL OZ/30ML) EXTRA-VIRGIN OLIVE OIL

2 GARLIC CLOVES, CRUSHED

SALT AND FRESHLY GROUND BLACK PEPPER

11/2 POUNDS (675G) FRESH SWORDFISH, CUT INTO 1-INCH (2.5-CM) CHUNKS

12 BAMBOO SKEWERS

2 ANCHOVY FILLETS, SOAKED IN COLD WATER FOR 10 MINUTES,
    PATTED DRY, AND MINCED

1/3 CUP (2 OZ/60G) IMPORTED GREEN OLIVES, SUCH AS PICHOLINE, PITTED
    AND CHOPPED

1/3 CUP (2 OZ/60G) IMPORTED BLACK OLIVES, SUCH AS KALAMATA OR
    NIÇOISE, CHOPPED

1/3 CUP (2 OZ/60G) SPANISH GREEN OLIVES WITH PIMIENTO, CHOPPED

1 GARLIC CLOVE, MINCED

1/2 CUP (1 OZ/30G) CHOPPED FRESH FLAT-LEAF PARSLEY

1 TABLESPOON WHITE WINE VINEGAR

6 LEMON WEDGES

WHOLE LEAVES OF FRESH FLAT-LEAF PARSLEY AS A GARNISH

With a vegetable peeler, peel the lemons into long strips, avoiding the pith. In a large dish, combine the strips of lemon peel, 2 tablespoons of the olive oil, the crushed garlic, and salt and pepper. Add the swordfish chunks, toss to coat, cover and refrigerate for 2 hours.

Juice the lemons and soak the bamboo skewers in half of the lemon juice for 1 hour. Reserve the remaining juice.

Heat a charcoal grill.

In a small bowl combine the anchovies, olives, garlic, parsley, vinegar, the reserved lemon juice, and the remaining 6 tablespoons olive oil. Season to taste with salt and pepper.

Skewer the swordfish. Grill the skewers, turning every 2 minutes until cooked but still slightly pink inside, about 6 to 7 minutes total.

Remove the swordfish skewers from the grill and place on a platter. Spoon the relish over the skewers and garnish with lemon wedges and parsley.

SERVES 6

I love the kitchen, but I'm not one to spend hours and hours laboring over a dish or recipe. Instead I like dishes with lots of flavor, focusing on the best ingredients, that are simple to prepare. That's what this dish is all about. Serve with a California Syrah, a wine that pairs so well with olives.

Crisp Salmon
with Green Herb and Caper Sauce

This technique for cooking salmon is fantastic, and yet it's so easy. All you need is a nonstick pan, a thin film of oil on the bottom of the pan, high heat, and a few fillets of freshly caught salmon. The outside of the fish is crisp and golden, while the inside is moist and tender.

$1/2$ CUP ($1/2$ OZ/15G) FRESH CHOPPED FLAT-LEAF PARSLEY
3 TABLESPOONS ($1/4$ OZ/8G) FRESH CHOPPED CHIVES
$1/2$ TEASPOON CHOPPED FRESH THYME
$1/2$ TEASPOON CHOPPED FRESH OREGANO
$1/4$ TEASPOON CHOPPED FRESH ROSEMARY
$1/4$ TEASPOON CHOPPED FRESH SAGE
3 TABLESPOONS (1 OZ/30G) CAPERS, CHOPPED
2 GARLIC CLOVES, MINCED
$1/2$ CUP (4 FL OZ/120ML) EXTRA-VIRGIN OLIVE OIL
SALT AND FRESHLY GROUND BLACK PEPPER
6 PIECES OF SALMON FILLET, SKIN REMOVED, ABOUT 2 POUNDS (1.8KG)
3 TABLESPOONS ($1 1/2$ FL OZ/45ML) LEMON JUICE
6 LEMON WEDGES AS A GARNISH

In a bowl, stir together the parsley, chives, thyme, oregano, rosemary, sage, capers, garlic and 6 tablespoons of the olive oil. Season to taste with salt and pepper.

Heat the remaining 2 tablespoons of olive oil over high heat in a large nonstick pan. Add the salmon in a single layer and cook until golden and crisp on 1 side, about 3 minutes. Turn the salmon carefully, season with salt and pepper, and continue to cook until golden and crisp on the second side, 2 to 3 minutes.

In the meantime, add the lemon juice to the green herb and caper sauce. To serve, place 1 salmon fillet on each plate and top with the herb and caper sauce. Garnish with lemon wedges and serve immediately.

SERVES 6

Salmon with Asparagus and Blood Oranges

1 NAVEL ORANGE

1 TEASPOON GRATED FRESH GINGER

2 TABLESPOONS BALSAMIC VINEGAR

1 TABLESPOON WHITE WINE VINEGAR

3 TABLESPOONS (1^1/$_2$ FL OZ/45 ML) EXTRA-VIRGIN OLIVE OIL

SALT AND FRESHLY GROUND BLACK PEPPER

3 BLOOD ORANGES

1^1/$_2$ POUNDS (675 G) ASPARAGUS, ENDS TRIMMED, CUT INTO
    2-INCH (5-CM) PIECES

6 SALMON FILLETS, 6 OUNCES (180 G) EACH

Grate the peel of 1 navel orange to make 1 teaspoon zest. Place the zest in a small bowl. Juice the navel orange and add it to the zest along with the ginger, balsamic vinegar, white wine vinegar, and olive oil. Season to taste with salt and pepper and set aside.

Cut the tops and bottoms off of the blood oranges. With a knife, cut off all of the peel so that no white pith remains. Cut the oranges across into ^{1}/$_4$-inch (0.6-cm) slices. Remove any seeds.

Bring a large saucepan of salted water to a boil. Add the asparagus and cook until tender yet crisp, 3 to 4 minutes.

Oil the salmon lightly. Heat a ridged grill over medium-high until heat for about 5 minutes.

Grill the salmon, skin side down, until golden and crisp, 3 to 4 minutes. Turn the salmon, season with salt and pepper, and continue to cook until done, 2 to 3 additional minutes.

Place the salmon in the middle of the plate. Place the asparagus and orange slices around the salmon. Drizzle the vinaigrette over the salmon, asparagus, and oranges, distributing evenly.

SERVES 6

Seasonal cooking is so basic. The foods that grow together most often go together. Think of strawberries and rhubarb, peas and fresh mint. South of San Francisco, the blood orange season is in full swing just as the tender shoots of asparagus are pushing their way to the surface. If blood oranges are unavailable, substitute navel oranges.

Grilled Sea Bass with Almond Romesco

When I see freshly caught fish, I immediately want to grill it over hardwood in my Tuscan oven or outdoors on a charcoal grill. Hot from the embers, the skin is crisp and the flesh falls from the bone. You can make the sauce early in the day, and at the end, simply grill the fish.

3 MEDIUM, RIPE RED TOMATOES

4 GARLIC CLOVES, UNPEELED

2 DRIED CHILES, SUCH AS ANCHOS

$1/_4$ TEASPOON CRUSHED RED PEPPER FLAKES

5 TABLESPOONS ($2^1/_2$ FL OZ/75ML) RED WINE VINEGAR

4 TABLESPOONS (2 FL OZ/60ML) EXTRA-VIRGIN OLIVE OIL

1 SLICE COARSE-TEXTURED COUNTRY-STYLE WHITE BREAD

12 ALMONDS, SKINS REMOVED

12 HAZELNUTS, SKINS REMOVED

$3/_4$ TEASPOON SWEET PAPRIKA

SALT AND FRESHLY GROUND BLACK PEPPER

2 WHOLE STRIPED BASS OR OTHER FIRM WHITE FISH, GUTTED AND SCALED, WASHED AND PATTED DRY, ABOUT $1^1/_2$ TO $1^3/_4$ POUNDS (675 TO 750G) EACH, OR 6 FILLETS, 6 TO 8 OUNCES (180 TO 225G) EACH

FLAT-LEAF PARSLEY AS A GARNISH

Preheat the oven to 350°F (175°C). Place the tomatoes and garlic in a roasting pan and bake about 30 minutes. Remove from the oven and peel, core, and seed the tomatoes. Peel the garlic and reserve both.

Place the dried chile and crushed red pepper in a saucepan with $1/_2$ cup (4 fl oz/125 ml) water and 3 tablespoons ($1^1/_2$ fl oz/45ml) of the vinegar. Bring to a boil over high heat, reduce to low, cover, and simmer slowly for 10 minutes. Turn the heat off and let steep 30 minutes. Strain peppers, discard seeds and liquid, and finely chop them.

Heat 1 tablespoon of the oil in a small skillet and fry the bread until golden. Transfer to a food processor. Add another 1 tablespoon oil to the pan and fry the almonds and hazelnuts until golden, 1 to 2 minutes. Add the nuts to the processor with the peppers, garlic, tomato, and paprika. With motor running, gradually pour in the remaining 2 table-spoons olive oil, 2 tablespoons vinegar, and salt and pepper, and puree until smooth. Strain through a coarse mesh strainer. Let sit at room temperature for 1 hour.

Preheat an outdoor grill. Brush the fish lightly with oil. Grill the fish, 4 inches (10cm) from the coals, until golden on 1 side, 6 to 7 minutes. Turn the fish and continue to cook until golden and cooked, 6 to 7 minutes. The fish is done when the thickest part reaches 140°F (60°C).

To serve, place the fish on a platter and spoon the sauce over the top. Garnish with whole sprigs of parsley and serve immediately.

SERVES 6

Oyster, Fennel, and Leek Stew

2 DOZEN FRESH OYSTERS IN THEIR SHELLS

3 TABLESPOONS ($1^1/_2$ OZ/45G) UNSALTED BUTTER

1 MEDIUM YELLOW ONION, CUT INTO $^1/_2$-INCH (1.25-CM) DICE

5 LARGE LEEKS, WHITE AND 2 INCHES OF GREEN,
   IN $^1/_2$-INCH (1.25-CM) SLICES

4 CELERY STALKS, CUT INTO $^1/_2$-INCH (1.25-CM) SLICES

2 FENNEL BULBS, CUT INTO $^1/_2$-INCH (1.25-CM) DICE,
   TOPS RESERVED AND CHOPPED AS A GARNISH

3 CUPS (24 FL OZ/700ML) BOTTLED CLAM JUICE OR FISH STOCK

$1^1/_2$ POUNDS (65G) POTATOES, PEELED AND CUT INTO $^1/_2$-INCH
   (1.25-CM) CUBES

$^1/_2$ CUP (4 FL OZ/120ML) HEAVY CREAM

2 TEASPOONS LEMON JUICE

SALT AND FRESHLY GROUND BLACK PEPPER

CELERY LEAVES AS A GARNISH

Shuck the oysters and reserve them separately from the oyster liquor. Discard the shells.

Melt the butter in a soup pot over medium-low heat. Add the onions, leeks, celery, and fennel and cook until the vegetables begin to soften, 10 to 15 minutes. Add the clam juice, 2 cups (16 fl oz/480ml) of water, and the potatoes and simmer until the vegetables are tender, about 15 minutes.

Remove one-quarter of the soup and puree in a blender on high speed until it is very smooth, about 3 minutes. Strain in a fine mesh strainer and return the pureed mixture to the soup base. Stir in the cream and lemon juice and season to taste with salt and pepper.

Just before serving the soup, place over medium heat, stirring occasionally, until very hot. Add the oysters and their liquor and simmer for 1 minute. Ladle the soup into bowls and garnish with chopped celery leaves and fennel greens.

SERVES 6

This stew is perfect for a winter dinner in front of the fireplace. It is made with fennel, leeks, celery, and potatoes, and I puree a bit of it to give it a rich texture without having to add much cream. Then just before serving, I poach fresh oysters in the stew. Don't forget a bottle of icy cold champagne!

Have you noticed how more and more restaurant menus are reading like a cross between a road atlas and a farmer's almanac? Scan the specials board at any corner café in San Francisco and you're likely to find a salad of Star Route baby greens, sugar snap peas from Green Gulch Farm, or a chutney made with Frog Hollow peaches.

I'm not complaining, mind you. I find this trend reassuring. I like knowing a little bit about where my food comes from before I eat it. After all, it's not unusual to choose a wine by its vineyard, so why not a fava bean by its farm?

When it comes to meat, most of the beef, pork, and lamb featured at my favorite Northern California restaurants carries a now-familiar pedigree: Niman Ranch. Founded in the mid-1970s by rancher Bill Niman and his neighbor, Orville Schell (a writer who has since left the business and gone on to become the dean of the U.C. Berkeley School of Journalism), Niman Ranch quickly became a favorite source for chefs like Alice Waters at Chez Panisse, Judy Rogers at Zuni Café, and Margaret Fox at Café Beaujolais. As demand from other restaurants grew, so did the business. Today, it's not only a cattle ranch based in West Marin County, it's also the distribution company for a network of sustainable family farms on which cattle, pigs, and sheep are raised in pastures on a diet of grass and all-natural corn and grain.

When I was cooking in restaurants, I used to pray that there would be one or two stray Niman steaks or lamb chops left over at the end of the shift that I could take home and grill. Nowadays, the meat is showcased on menus all over Northern California and sold in a few specialty food stores. The other day, I even stumbled across a Philadelphia cheese-steak shop a few miles from my house whose menu board proudly boasts: "Our sandwiches are made with the finest Niman Ranch beef." Only in San Francisco!

Over in Berkeley, Marsha McBride is working

of the Matter

Above and opposite: Northern California is heaven on earth for cooks,
with many farms providing wonderful fresh food.

wonders with Niman Ranch meats at Café Rouge, her stylish restaurant with a "meat-intensive" menu and a meat counter and charcuterie right in the back of the dining room. You can sit down to a great steak with crisp fries, and, on your way out, pick up a few pounds of Niman Ranch beef, a couple of lamb chops from Marsha's cousin Jeanne McCormack's sheep ranch, or some house-made salami, prosciutto, or sausages to take home. Marsha loves to watch the customer's reactions when they walk into the restaurant and spy the meat case. Some are a little taken aback when

they see all that red meat on display. But generally, she says, the response has been enthusiastic and business has been brisk. There are even some regulars who sit at the bar nursing a Manhattan, chatting with the meat cutters and admiring the merchandise. "I guess it's a guy thing, kind of like looking at cars," she tells me.

It's been really interesting watching Niman Ranch and Café Rouge grow. They're more than just businesses. They're pioneers who have done so much to educate people about meat and responsible agriculture, reminding us all to enjoy what we eat instead of being afraid of it.

By this point, you've probably realized that I'm an enthusiastic carnivore. (Maybe it's because I love any excuse to enjoy a great glass of red wine.) On trip after trip to Italy, Spain, France, Morocco, and Greece, I've found that the meat and poultry dishes that I love best are often the simplest ones—a juicy steak grilled over hot embers and finished with a good dose of lemon juice; spit-roasted lamb and pork brushed with herbs and olive oil; slowly braised stews with meltingly tender meat and assertive seasonings. Back in California, that's how I satisfy my carnivorous cravings. Nothing fancy. Nothing contrived. Nothing to interfere with the real meat of the matter. It suits my style of living and my style of cooking.

A small farm in Sonoma County, California.

Chicken Breasts
Stuffed with Goat Cheese and Olives

4 OUNCES (120G) FRESH GOAT CHEESE

1 TABLESPOON WHOLE MILK

2 GARLIC CLOVES, MINCED

1 TABLESPOON CHOPPED FLAT-LEAF PARSLEY

1 TEASPOON CHOPPED FRESH OREGANO

1 TEASPOON CHOPPED FRESH THYME

PINCH OF DRIED RED PEPPER FLAKES

2 TABLESPOONS CHOPPED IMPORTED BLACK OLIVES, SUCH AS
    KALAMATA OR NIÇOISE

SALT AND FRESHLY GROUND BLACK PEPPER

6 BONELESS, SKINLESS CHICKEN BREAST HALVES, ABOUT
    6 OUNCES (180G) EACH

2 TABLESPOONS EXTRA-VIRGIN OLIVE OIL

$1/2$ CUP (4 FL OZ/120ML) DRY WHITE WINE, SUCH AS SAUVIGNON BLANC

$1/2$ CUP (4 FL OZ/120ML) CHICKEN STOCK

In a small bowl, mash together the goat cheese and milk until smooth. Add the garlic, parsley, oregano, thyme, and red pepper flakes. Mix in the olives and season to taste with salt and pepper.

On the thickest side of each chicken breast, cut a deep, 3-inch (7.5-cm) long pocket. Using your fingers, stuff the goat cheese mixture into each pocket. Close by pressing the flesh together and secure with a toothpick, if necessary.

In a large frying pan, heat the oil over medium heat. Have ready a lid that is too small for the pan but will cover all the breasts. Cook the chicken on one side until golden brown, 4 to 5 minutes. Turn the breasts, season with salt and pepper and set the small lid on top of the chicken in the pan. Continue to cook until the chicken is cooked through, 4 to 5 minutes more.

Transfer the chicken to a warm serving platter. Pour the wine into the pan and cook, scraping up the flavorful brown bits stuck to the bottom of the pan. Cook until the wine has reduced by about half, 1 to 2 minutes. Add the chicken stock, season with salt and pepper, and cook until the sauce is reduced to a glossy syrup, about 1 minute. Drizzle the reduction over the chicken and serve.

SERVES 6

Boneless, skinless chicken breasts are a great starting point for a simple weeknight dinner. Or gussied up with a gratin of potatoes or garlic mashed potatoes, they are fine for weekend entertaining. But when you remove the skin and bone from the chicken, you've lost a lot of the flavor. So they need something to give them a little jump start in the flavor direction. I like to stuff chicken breasts with fresh goat cheese, imported black olives, and—from the garden—freshly picked oregano, flat-leaf parsley, and thyme. Get them ready several hours ahead of time and cook them at the last minute.

Grilled Chicken Breasts
with Sweet Corn and Pepper Relish

It's the height of summer, you wander into your garden, and it seems that almost overnight sweet bell peppers in jewel-like colors have overrun the garden. What to do? Make a pepper and corn relish to serve with just about every meat or fish available—grilled chicken breasts, halibut, swordfish, tuna, pork chops, lamb chops, or rib-eye steaks.

1 LEMON

6 BONELESS, SKINLESS CHICKEN BREAST HALVES,
   ABOUT 6 OUNCES (180G) EACH

6 TABLESPOONS (3 FL OZ/100ML) EXTRA-VIRGIN OLIVE OIL

1 EAR FRESH CORN, KERNELS REMOVED FROM THE COB, ABOUT 1 CUP

1 RED BELL PEPPER, HALVED, CORED, AND CUT INTO
   $1/4$-INCH (0.6-CM) DICE

1 GREEN BELL PEPPER, HALVED, CORED, AND CUT INTO
   $1/4$-INCH (0.6-CM) DICE

1 YELLOW BELL PEPPER, HALVED, CORED, AND CUT INTO
   $1/4$-INCH (0.6-CM) DICE

1 SMALL RED ONION, CUT INTO $1/4$-INCH (0.6-CM) DICE

2 GARLIC CLOVES, MINCED

3 TABLESPOONS ($1/4$ OZ/8G) CHOPPED FRESH FLAT-LEAF PARSLEY

$1/4$ CUP (2 FL OZ/60ML) RED WINE VINEGAR

SALT AND FRESHLY GROUND BLACK PEPPER

WHOLE LEAVES FLAT-LEAF PARSLEY AS A GARNISH

Peel the lemon with a vegetable peeler. Marinate the chicken breasts in the refrigerator with 2 tablespoons olive oil and lemon peel for 2 hours or overnight.

Bring a small saucepan of salted water to a boil Add the corn and simmer for 1 minute. Drain and let cool.

To make the relish, combine the corn, red, green, and yellow peppers, onions, garlic, and parsley in a bowl. Mix thoroughly. Add the remaining 5 tablespoons (2 oz/60g) olive oil and vinegar. Season to taste with salt and pepper.

Preheat a charcoal grill.

Grill the chicken breasts until golden on 1 side, 4 to 5 minutes. Turn the breasts, season with salt and pepper, and continue to grill until golden and cooked through, 4 to 5 minutes.

To serve, slice each chicken breast on the diagonal into 4 to 5 slices. Top with the relish and garnish with parsley leaves.

SERVES 6

Chicken Ragout with Autumn Vegetables

2 TABLESPOONS UNSALTED BUTTER

4 (4 OZ/120G) BACON SLICES, CUT INTO $1/2$-INCH (1.25-CM) DICE

1 WHOLE CHICKEN, ABOUT 4 POUNDS (1.7KG), CUT INTO 10 PIECES

SALT AND FRESHLY GROUND BLACK PEPPER

4 CUPS (32 FL OZ/950ML) DRY WHITE WINE, SUCH AS SAUVIGNON BLANC

4 CUPS (32 FL OZ/950ML) CHICKEN STOCK

3 GARLIC CLOVES, MINCED

2 BAY LEAVES

$1/2$ TEASPOON CHOPPED FRESH THYME

6 PARSLEY SPRIGS, TIED TOGETHER

2 PARSNIPS, PEELED AND CUT INTO 1-INCH (2.5-CM) LENGTHS

2 CARROTS, PEELED AND CUT INTO 1-INCH (2.5-CM) LENGTHS

1 MEDIUM TURNIP, PEELED AND CUT INTO 8 WEDGES

1 MEDIUM RUTABAGA, PEELED AND CUT INTO 8 WEDGES

2 TABLESPOONS ALL-PURPOSE FLOUR

1 TABLESPOON COARSELY CHOPPED FRESH FLAT-LEAF PARSLEY

Melt 1 tablespoon butter in a large, heavy casserole over medium heat. Add the bacon and cook until light golden, about 10 minutes. Remove with a slotted spoon and set aside. Increase the heat to medium high. In the same pan, add the chicken in a single layer with space between and cook until light golden on each side, 10 minutes. Remove the white meat. Add the bacon and mix well. Increase the heat to high and add the wine, stock, garlic, bay leaves, thyme, and parsley. Bring to a boil, reduce the heat to low, and simmer, covered, for 15 minutes. Place the white meat back in the pan and continue to cook until the chicken is done, 5 to 10 minutes. Remove the chicken from the pan with tongs and set aside, covered with foil to keep warm.

Strain the liquid and pour it back into the pan. Discard the solids. Add the parsnips, carrots, turnip, and rutabaga, cover, and cook until the vegetables are tender, about 15 minutes. With a slotted spoon, remove the vegetables from the pan. Increase the heat to high and reduce the broth until 3 cups remain, 5 to 8 minutes. Skim.

In a small bowl, mash together the flour and remaining 1 tablespoon butter with a fork. Bring the liquid to a boil and, with a whisk, mix the flour and butter into the liquid, simmering until the liquid thickens and coats a spoon lightly, 2 to 3 minutes.

To serve, heat the sauce over medium high heat until it is hot. Add the chicken and vegetables and heat through, 3 to 4 minutes. Place the vegetables and chicken on a platter and drizzle the sauce over the top. Garnish with parsley and serve.

SERVES 4 TO 6

Autumn brings to mind make-shift vegetable stands set up along country roads. Signs scrawled with chicken-scratch hand-lettering boasted butternut squash, carrots, parsnips, rutabagas, and turnips. I remember when I was a kid, my mother and I would always stop and buy baskets of winter vegetables, which she would store in the cellar where the temperature was a constant 55°F (13°C) throughout the winter. For the next few months, these winter vegetables would show up in all kinds of soups and stews. These hearty dishes taste just as good during a chilly Napa Valley winter.

Herb-Roasted Chicken Cooked under a Brick

1 WHOLE CHICKEN, 3$\frac{1}{2}$ TO 4 POUNDS (1.5 TO 1.7KG)

3 TABLESPOONS ($\frac{1}{4}$ OZ/8G) CHOPPED FRESH FLAT-LEAF PARSLEY

2 TABLESPOONS SNIPPED FRESH CHIVES

1 TABLESPOON CHOPPED FRESH LEMON VERBENA (OPTIONAL)

1$\frac{1}{2}$ TEASPOONS CHOPPED FRESH THYME

1$\frac{1}{2}$ TEASPOONS CHOPPED FRESH OREGANO

2 TABLESPOONS EXTRA-VIRGIN OLIVE OIL

1 TEASPOON GRATED LEMON ZEST

SALT AND FRESHLY GROUND BLACK PEPPER

SPRIGS OF THYME AND PARSLEY, AS A GARNISH

*L*eave it to the Italians to come up with an ingenious way to cook chicken perfectly. But under a brick? First you want to flatten a chicken by cutting down the backbone. Tuck a savory stuffing between the flesh and the skin and grill it under a baking sheet topped with a couple of bricks. The chicken ends up as flat as a pancake, the meat as moist as can be, and the skin is incredibly crisp.

Cut off the wing tips to the second joint and set aside for making stock. Cut down both sides of the backbone to remove the backbone. Place the backbone with the wing tips. Remove the excess fat. Flatten the chicken as best you can by pressing on the breast.

Preheat a charcoal grill.

In a small bowl, combine the parsley, chives, lemon verbena, thyme, oregano, olive oil, and lemon zest. Season to taste with salt and pepper. Separate the skin from the breasts and legs of the chicken. Slide the herb mixture between the skin and the meat of the chicken.

Place the skin side of the chicken on the grill set about 4 inches from the coals. Top with a baking sheet. Place a brick on top of the baking sheet and let cook until golden brown, 15 to 20 minutes more. Remove the bricks and baking sheet and turn the chicken. Continue to cook until the chicken is done, 15 to 20 minutes. Remove from the grill and cover with foil for 10 minutes.

To serve, cut the chicken into pieces, garnish with herbs, and serve immediately.

SERVES 4 TO 6

Penne with Tomatoes, Spicy Fennel Sausage, and Cream

1 TABLESPOON EXTRA-VIRGIN OLIVE OIL

1 POUND (450G) SWEET ITALIAN PORK AND FENNEL SAUSAGE, CRUMBLED

1 SMALL RED ONION, CHOPPED

2 GARLIC CLOVES, MINCED

PINCH OF CRUSHED RED PEPPER FLAKES

2 BAY LEAVES

1 TEASPOON CHOPPED FRESH SAGE

1 TEASPOON CHOPPED FRESH ROSEMARY

$^3/_4$ CUP (6 FL OZ/180ML) DRY RED WINE

$2^1/_2$ CUPS (20 OZ/600G) PEELED, SEEDED, AND DICED TOMATOES, FRESH OR CANNED

$^3/_4$ CUP (6 FL OZ/180ML) HEAVY CREAM

$^3/_4$ CUP (3 OZ/90G) GRATED PARMIGIANO REGGIANO CHEESE

SALT AND FRESHLY GROUND BLACK PEPPER

12 OUNCES (350G) DRIED PENNE OR RIGATONI

So many different types of sausage are available at the market today! Frequently, the whole display case is filled and the array provides inspiration for scores of dishes. This pasta, an all-time favorite, is made with spicy hot pork sausage flavored with fennel seeds. Often I only find this sausage available in casings. If so, remove it from the casings and crumble.

Heat the olive oil in a large frying pan over medium heat. Add the sausage and cook until the fat is rendered and the juices have evaporated, 8 to 10 minutes. Add the onions, garlic, crushed red pepper flakes, bay leaves, sage, and rosemary, and cook, stirring occasionally, until the onions are soft, about 15 minutes. Drain off all but 2 tablespoons of fat and discard. Turn the heat to high, add the wine and boil until it has almost evaporated, 5 minutes. Add the tomatoes and bring to a boil. Reduce the heat to low and simmer until the sauce thickens, 30 to 40 minutes. Remove the bay leaves and discard. Add the cream and half of the Parmigiano Reggiano and stir together. Season to taste with salt and pepper.

Bring a large pot of salted water to a boil. Add the penne and cook until al dente, 10 to 12 minutes or according to the directions on the package. Drain the pasta, put it back in the pan, and toss with the tomato sauce. Place on a platter, sprinkle with the remaining Parmigiano Reggiano, and serve immediately.

SERVES 6

Pork Chops with Asparagus and Morels

1/4 OUNCE (8G) DRIED MOREL MUSHROOMS (OR OTHER
DRIED WILD MUSHROOMS)
3/4 POUND (350G) ASPARAGUS, ENDS TRIMMED,
CUT INTO 1 1/2-INCH (4-CM) LENGTHS
2 TABLESPOONS EXTRA-VIRGIN OLIVE OIL
6 CENTER-CUT PORK CHOPS, EACH ABOUT 6 OUNCES (180G)
AND 1 INCH (2.5CM) THICK, TRIMMED OF EXCESS FAT
SALT AND FRESHLY GROUND BLACK PEPPER
1 1/2 CUPS (12 FL OZ/360ML) CHICKEN STOCK
1/2 POUND (240G) FRESH MOREL MUSHROOMS (OR OTHER
WILD MUSHROOMS), HALVED
1 TEASPOON CHOPPED FRESH THYME
THYME SPRIGS AS A GARNISH

Spring showers mean wild mushrooms to foragers. They feverishly tromp through the woods where they find morels and other delights. Thin-fleshed, brown in color, morels are shaped like a round hollow cone with honeycomb-like ridges. Combined with asparagus and pork chops, the flavors are delicate, earthy, and nutty. If morels are unavailable, substitute any other edible wild or cultivated mushrooms.

In a small bowl, combine 1/2 cup (4 fl oz/120ml) boiling water and the dried morels. Let cool to room temperature, about 20 minutes. Line a strainer with cheesecloth and drain the mushrooms. Chop the mushrooms and reserve the mushrooms and their liquid separately.

Bring a saucepan of salted water to a boil. Add the asparagus and cook until tender yet crisp, 3 to 5 minutes. Drain and reserve.

In a frying pan large enough to hold the chops in a single layer without crowding, warm 1 tablespoon of the olive oil over medium heat. Add the pork chops and cook, uncovered, for 5 minutes. Turn them over and season with salt and pepper. Reduce the heat to medium-low and continue to cook, uncovered, turning occasionally, until golden and firm to the touch, about 8 to 9 minutes longer. Remove from the pan, place on a warm platter, and cover with aluminum foil.

Pour the chicken stock into a saucepan and boil rapidly to reduce by half. Set aside.

In the frying pan used to cook the pork chops, heat the remaining 1 tablespoon olive oil over medium-high heat. Add the fresh and dried morels and cook until the fresh mushrooms are tender, 3 to 4 minutes. Remove the mushrooms from the pan and reserve with the pork. Turn the heat to high, add the chicken stock, thyme, and mushroom liquid and reduce until it thickens slightly, 3 to 5 minutes. Add the reserved asparagus and warm for 1 minute.

Place the pork chops on individual plates and divide the sauce, asparagus, and mushrooms over the top. Garnish with thyme sprigs and serve.

SERVES 6

Pork and Artichoke Stew

1 LEMON

6 MEDIUM-SIZE ARTICHOKES

3 TABLESPOONS (1¹/₂ FL OZ/45ML) EXTRA-VIRGIN OLIVE OIL

2 MEDIUM YELLOW ONIONS, CHOPPED

3 POUNDS (1.3KG) PORK BUTT, FAT REMOVED, CUT INTO
    2-INCH (5-CM) CUBES

1¹/₂ TABLESPOONS FLOUR

SALT AND FRESHLY GROUND BLACK PEPPER

2 TEASPOONS CHOPPED FRESH OREGANO

3 GARLIC CLOVES, CHOPPED

1 CUP (8 FL OZ/240ML) DRY WHITE WINE, SUCH AS SAUVIGNON BLANC

1¹/₂ CUPS (12 OZ/350G) PEELED, SEEDED, AND CHOPPED TOMATOES

3 CUPS (24 FL OZ/700ML) CHICKEN STOCK

OREGANO SPRIGS AS A GARNISH

My French friend, Magaly, makes terrific Chateauneuf-du-Pape wines with her husband, Raymond. When I think of her, I can't help but think about the knack she has not only for making world-class wine, but also for taking simple things like pork and artichokes and turning them into something irresistible. One Sunday she invited me to lunch at her house in the Vaucluse in the south of France, and she served this stew of tender chunks of pork, spring artichokes, oregano, and her own canned tomatoes, accompanied, of course, by a bottle of their own wine.

Have ready a large bowl of water to which you have added the juice of the lemon. Remove the tough outer leaves of the artichokes. Cut off the top half of the artichokes including all of the prickly leaf points. Remove the tough outer leaves of the artichoke until you get to the very light green leaves. Pare the stem to reveal the light green center. Cut in half lengthwise, then scoop out the prickly chokes and discard. Cut in half again. As each is cut, place in the bowl of lemon water.

Warm 1 tablespoon of the olive oil in a large skillet over medium heat. Drain the artichokes and add them to the pan, along with ¹/4 cup (2 fl oz/60ml) water. Cover and cook, stirring occasionally, until the artichokes are almost tender, 15 to 20 minutes. Remove and reserve.

Warm 1 tablespoon of the olive oil in a large, heavy casserole and cook the onions, stirring occasionally, until light golden, 15 minutes. Remove with a slotted spoon and set aside.

Add the remaining 1 tablespoon olive oil to the pan. Over medium-high heat, add the pork in a single layer. Do not overcrowd the pan. Cook, turning occasionally, until golden on all sides, 7 to 10 minutes. Sprinkle the pork with the flour and salt and pepper, and continue to cook until the flour is light golden. Return the onions to the pan with the oregano and garlic. Add the wine and cook until it reduces by half, 3 minutes. Add the tomatoes and chicken stock and bring to a boil over high heat. Reduce the heat to low and simmer, covered, until the pork is tender, 1¹/2 to 2 hours. Add the artichokes and season to taste with salt and pepper. Simmer slowly for 2 minutes. Ladle the stew into soup bowls, garnish with oregano, and serve immediately.

SERVES 6

Pork Tenderloin with Onion, Orange, and Raisin Marmalade

2 LARGE PORK TENDERLOINS, ABOUT 1 POUND (450G) EACH

3 TABLESPOONS (1$^{1}/_{2}$ FL OZ/45ML) EXTRA-VIRGIN OLIVE OIL

$^{1}/_{4}$ TEASPOON PAPRIKA

$^{1}/_{4}$ TEASPOON GROUND CUMIN

$^{1}/_{4}$ TEASPOON GROUND CLOVES

LARGE PINCH OF CAYENNE

SALT AND FRESHLY GROUND BLACK PEPPER

1 NAVEL ORANGE

$^{1}/_{3}$ CUP (2 OZ/60G) GOLDEN RAISINS

$^{1}/_{4}$ CUP (2 FL OZ/60ML) SHERRY VINEGAR

2 MEDIUM YELLOW ONIONS, THINLY SLICED

2 TEASPOONS SUGAR

$^{1}/_{2}$ CUP (4 FL OZ/120ML) DRY WHITE WINE, SUCH AS SAUVIGNON BLANC

2 CUPS (16 FL OZ/475ML) CHICKEN STOCK

3 SPRIGS OF FRESH PARSLEY

2 BAY LEAVES

8 WHOLE CLOVES

Butterfly the pork by slitting lengthwise just far enough so it opens up to make a flat piece. Flatten slightly. In a bowl, combine 1 tablespoon olive oil, paprika, cumin, cloves, cayenne, and pepper. Rub it over the pork, place in a baking dish, cover, and refrigerate 2 hours or overnight.

Zest the orange to make 1 teaspoon grated zest. Juice the orange. In a small saucepan, combine the orange zest, orange juice, raisins, and sherry vinegar. Simmer very slowly, uncovered, for 10 minutes. Heat the remaining 2 tablespoon olive oil in a large skillet over medium heat. Add the onions and cook, stirring occasionally, until very soft, about 20 minutes. Add the raisin mixture, sprinkle with sugar, cover, and continue to sauté very slowly until the onions are very soft, 30 minutes. Add $^{1}/_{4}$ cup (2 fl oz/60ml) water and continue to cook uncovered until almost dry, 20 minutes. Season to taste with salt and pepper. Place the pork on a work surface, cut side up. Season with salt. Spread the onion mixture evenly over the flattened pork. Close up the pork so it is its original shape and tie at 1-inch (2.5-cm) intervals with kitchen string.

In a large skillet, bring the white wine, chicken stock, parsley, bay leaf, and whole cloves to a boil. Add the pork, reduce the heat to low, and simmer until the pork is done, 25 to 30 minutes. Remove the pork and keep warm. Reduce the stock by half and strain. Season with salt and pepper. Remove strings and slice meat into 3/4-inch (2-cm) slices. Place on a platter and drizzle the sauce on top before serving.

SERVES 6

I often serve this stuffed pork tenderloin to guests, because I can prepare it well in advance. Trim the pork of all fat and cut it to lay flat on your work surface. Make an aromatic stuffing of stewed onions, golden raisins, orange, and plenty of spices. Spread the stuffing onto the pork, roll and tie the pork, and then braise it until it's fork tender.

A Purple Carpet

WHEN I THINK OF LAVENDER I can't help but be transported to the fields of Provence, where everything is scented with this aromatic flower.

But we have our own lavender right here in the Wine Country. Matanzas Creek Winery, without a doubt, is the most prolific, with a field of more than five hundred plants. But other vineyards, such as Beaulieu Vineyards and Robert Sinsky Vineyards, grow their share of this aromatic flower.

Beginning in June, the Wine Country is a sea of purple with lavender plants. These lovely flowers are not only used for shampoo, soap, and lotions, but they are also used for flavoring everything from delicious ice creams to savory lamb. It sounds strange, but lavender is a flavoring that can be used in both sweet and savory dishes. When I am cooking with lamb, I love the flavor of lavender with other fresh herbs like mint, parsley, chives, thyme, rosemary, and oregano, a kind of fresh *herbes de Provençe* mixture. I marinate the butterflied leg of lamb with the herbs overnight and then the next day, roll it, tie it, and roast it in the oven or spit roast it.

If you don't have access to fresh lavender flowers, you can always use dried flowers, but be sure that you buy lavender that is unsprayed. Perhaps the best place to find it is at a health food store or gourmet shop. And, of course, if you want to plant your own, remember that lavender doesn't need much water. It loves dry weather, heat, and sunshine, with just an occasional pruning. In those conditions, you will have the loveliest purple-colored carpet you can imagine.

Grilled Leg of Lamb with Lavender-Rosemary Rub

5- TO 6-POUND (2.3- TO 2.7-KG) LEG OF LAMB, BONED, EXCESS FAT REMOVED, AND BUTTERFLIED

3 GARLIC CLOVES, THINLY SLICED

2 TABLESPOONS DRY OR FRESH LAVENDER FLOWERS

3 TABLESPOONS (1/4 OZ/8G) CHOPPED FRESH ROSEMARY

2 TABLESPOONS CHOPPED FRESH MINT

3 TABLESPOONS (1 1/2 FL OZ/45ML) EXTRA-VIRGIN OLIVE OIL

SALT AND FRESHLY GROUND BLACK PEPPER

SPRIGS OF LAVENDER AS A GARNISH

Make 20 small incisions in the lamb in various places. Tuck a slice of garlic in each incision.

In a bowl, combine the lavender flowers, rosemary, mint, and olive oil. Rub the mixture over the lamb and let sit at room temperature for 2 hours, or overnight in the refrigerator.

Preheat a charcoal grill or broiler.

Place the lamb 4 inches (10cm) from the coals on the grill or under the broiler. Cook until 1 side is golden, about 15 minutes. Season well with salt and pepper. Turn the lamb and continue to cook until medium rare, 130 to 135°F (54 to 57°C) when tested with an instant-read thermometer, about 15 minutes. Test by cutting into the thickest part. If it is slightly pink inside, remove from the grill. Cover with foil and let rest 10 minutes.

Slice the lamb into thin slices across the grain and place on a platter. Garnish with lavender sprigs before serving.

Grilled Lamb on Rosemary Skewers with Warm Fava Salad

12 ROSEMARY SKEWERS (SEE HEADNOTE), 8- TO 10-INCHES
(20- TO 25-CM) LONG
4 POUNDS (3.6KG) FRESH FAVA BEANS IN THE PODS
5 TABLESPOONS (2$\frac{1}{2}$ FL OZ/75ML) EXTRA-VIRGIN OLIVE OIL
1 TEASPOON GRATED LEMON ZEST
2 TABLESPOONS LEMON JUICE
1 TABLESPOON CHOPPED FRESH MINT
SALT AND FRESHLY GROUND BLACK PEPPER
2$\frac{1}{2}$ POUNDS (1.2KG) LAMB CUBES, CUT FROM THE LEG OR LOIN,
TRIMMED OF ALL FAT
6 LEMON WEDGES AS A GARNISH
FRESH MINT SPRIGS AS A GARNISH

Soak the rosemary skewers in water for 30 minutes.

Remove the fava beans from their pods and discard. Bring a pot of water to a boil, add the fava beans, and boil for 30 seconds. Drain, cool, and shell the beans. Reserve.

In a bowl, whisk together 4 tablespoons (2 fl oz/60ml) of the olive oil, the lemon zest, lemon juice, and mint. Season to taste with salt and pepper. Add the fava beans and stir together.

Preheat a charcoal grill.

Thread the lamb on the rosemary skewers, distributing evenly. Brush the lamb with the remaining 1 tablespoon oil. Grill the lamb, turning occasionally, until the lamb is slightly firm to the touch, 6 to 8 minutes total.

To serve, place the fava beans on a platter. Top with the skewers of lamb. Garnish with lemon wedges and mint sprigs and serve immediately.

SERVES 6

Forget the bamboo skewers for this recipe. You can make these skewers yourself. Simply strip the rosemary leaves off the entire stem, except for about 1 inch (2.5cm) at the top. These skewers look great, hot from the grill, and the rosemary also flavors the pieces of lamb, beef, chicken, pork or fish from the inside.

Pot-Roasted Leg of Lamb
with Garlic and Olives

Years ago, Lulu Peyraud of Domaine Tempier in Bandol, a small farm near Marseilles, famous for its wine, made me this pot-roasted lamb that literally melted in my mouth. Instead of roasting the whole leg in the oven, she pot-roasted it slowly with white wine and plenty of garlic on top of the stove. At the end, she threw in a few handfuls of olives. Serve this with roasted potatoes, tender young green beans, and a gutsy red wine, such as Zinfandel, Pinot Noir, Syrah, or even Cabernet Sauvignon or Bandol.

3 TABLESPOONS (1^1/$_2$ FL OZ/45ML) EXTRA-VIRGIN OLIVE OIL
1 WHOLE LEG OF LAMB, 5^1/$_2$ TO 6 POUNDS (2.5 TO 2.7KG), BONE-IN
SALT AND FRESHLY GROUND BLACK PEPPER
1 LARGE YELLOW ONION, CHOPPED
1 CUP (8 OZ/240G) PEELED, SEEDED, AND CHOPPED TOMATOES,
    FRESH OR CANNED
24 GARLIC CLOVES, PEELED AND CRUSHED
5 SPRIGS OF FRESH THYME
1 CUP (8 FL OZ/240ML) DRY WHITE WINE, SUCH AS SAUVIGNON BLANC
1 CUP (6 OZ/180G) IMPORTED BLACK OLIVES, SUCH AS NIÇOISE
    OR KALAMATA

In a large heavy pot, warm the olive oil over medium heat. Season the lamb with salt and pepper. Add the lamb to the pan and cook, turning occasionally, until golden brown on all sides, about 30 minutes. Add the onions and, stirring occasionally, cook the onions until golden, about 20 minutes. Reduce the heat to low, add the tomatoes, garlic, thyme, and ^{1}/$_4$ cup (2 fl oz/60ml) of the wine, cover and cook, turning the lamb occasionally, for about 30 minutes. Add another ^{1}/$_4$ cup (2 fl oz/60ml) wine and continue to cook for 30 minutes. Add the olives and another ^{1}/$_4$ cup (2 fl oz/60ml) wine and continue to cook, turning the lamb occasionally, for 30 minutes more. Repeat 1 more time.

After 2 hours total cooking time, remove the lamb from the pot, cover with foil, and let rest for 10 minutes. Remove and discard the thyme.

To serve, slice the lamb and place on a platter. Spoon the garlic and sauce over the lamb. Serve immediately, passing the remaining sauce separately.

SERVES 6 TO 8

Golden Veal with Arugula and Tomato Salad

1¹/₄ POUNDS (500G) VEAL SCALLOPINE, CUT FROM THE SIRLOIN
SALT AND FRESHLY GROUND BLACK PEPPER
2 EGGS, BEATEN LIGHTLY TOGETHER
¹/₂ CUP (2 OZ/60G) ALL-PURPOSE FLOUR
2 CUPS (7 OZ/210G) DRY BREAD CRUMBS
5 TABLESPOONS (2¹/₂ FL OZ/75ML) EXTRA-VIRGIN OLIVE OIL
2 TABLESPOONS LEMON JUICE
1 SMALL GARLIC CLOVE, MINCED
2 TABLESPOONS UNSALTED BUTTER
3 CUPS (10 OZ/300G) VERY, VERY COARSELY CHOPPED ARUGULA
2 SMALL TOMATOES, CUT INTO ¹/₂-INCH (1.25-CM) DICE
LEMON WEDGES AS A GARNISH

Pound each piece of veal between two pieces of waxed paper or plastic wrap with a large flat meat pounder until the veal is ¹/₄-inch (0.6-cm) thick. To bread the veal, place the flour, eggs, and bread crumbs in three separate bowl. Season the flour and bread crumbs with salt and pepper and mix well. Coat both sides of the veal with flour, shaking off the excess. Next, coat the veal with egg, letting the excess drain. Coat both sides of the veal lightly with bread crumbs. Place on baking sheets in the refrigerator until just before serving.

In a small bowl, whisk together 3 tablespoons (1¹/₂ fl oz/45ml) of the olive oil, the lemon juice, and garlic. Season to taste with salt and pepper. Reserve.

In a large skillet, heat the remaining 2 tablespoons olive oil and butter over medium high heat. Add the veal pieces in a single layer. Do not overcrowd the pan. Sauté the veal pieces, turning occasionally, until they are golden brown on each side, 4 to 6 minutes total.

To serve, place the veal on a platter. Toss the arugula, tomatoes, and vinaigrette together. Top the veal with the salad and serve immediately, garnished with lemon wedges.

SERVES 6

Is this just an excuse to eat this salad of tomatoes and arugula tossed with lemon, garlic, and extra-virgin olive oil? Maybe so, because you can make the same dish with skinned and boned chicken breasts that have been pounded flat, and the salad is also a real treat as a topping on a hot-from-the-oven fontina and mozzarella pizza.

Grilled Veal Chops
with Olives, Capers, and Sage

Olive oil for frying

20 large sage leaves

2 tablespoons extra-virgin olive oil

6 rib-eye veal chops, about 8 to 10 ounces (240 to 300g) each

Salt and freshly ground black pepper

3 garlic cloves, minced

1 cup (8 fl oz/240ml) dry white wine

1 cup (6 oz/180g) imported black or green olives, pitted and very coarsely chopped

$^1/_4$ cup (1 oz/30g) capers

2 tablespoons chopped fresh sage

2 cups (16 fl oz/475ml) chicken stock

1 tablespoon lemon juice

If I see veal chops on a restaurant menu, I always want to order them. When you take robust flavors like cured olives, capers, sage, garlic, and lemon juice and pair them with veal, a fairly neutral meat, the veal takes on those wonderful flavors. This simple-to-prepare-at-the-last-moment dish is a great one for entertaining. You can always substitute boned chicken breasts for veal chops.

Warm $^1/_2$ inch olive oil in the bottom of a skillet over medium-high heat. When the oil is hot, add the sage leaves and cook until crisp, 30 to 60 seconds. Remove from the pan and drain on paper towels. Reserve for garnishing.

Heat 1 tablespoon of the olive oil in a large skillet over medium heat. Add the veal chops and cook until golden, 5 to 6 minutes. Turn the veal chops, season with salt and pepper, and continue to cook until golden and cooked to medium rare, 5 to 6 minutes. Remove from the pan, place on a warm platter, cover with foil, and keep warm.

Increase the heat to medium-high, add the remaining 1 tablespoon olive oil and the garlic, and cook until the garlic is soft, about 15 seconds. Add the white wine and simmer until the wine has almost evaporated, 3 to 5 minutes. Add the chicken stock and reduce by half, 3 to 5 minutes. Add the olives, capers, and fresh sage and stir together. Add the lemon juice and salt and pepper to taste.

To serve, place one chop on each plate and spoon the sauce, olives, and capers over the top and around the sides. Garnish with crisp sage leaves and serve immediately.

Serves 6

Beef Roulade with Roasted Fennel and Sweet Peppers

A ll over the wine country, wild fennel grows along the side of the road. Much to my dismay, it isn't the variety with the edible bulb; instead its aromatic yellow flowers perfume the air. I use the flowers to make an Italian digestif called finochetto or as a lovely garnish. If you love fennel as I do, you will love this dish. Stuff rib-eye steaks with finely diced fennel, carrots, celery, onions, and fennel seed, roll and tie, then braise and serve with roasted fennel and sweet red peppers. Roasted potatoes would make a terrific accompaniment.

2 POUNDS (900G) RIB-EYE STEAKS, $1^1/_2$ TO 2-INCHES (4 TO 5-CM)
   THICK, IN 2 PIECES
1 SMALL CARROT
$1/_2$ SMALL YELLOW ONION
1 CELERY STALK
1 SMALL FENNEL BULB
$1/_4$ CUP (2 FL OZ/60ML) OLIVE OIL
1 GARLIC CLOVE, MINCED
$3/_4$ TEASPOON CRUSHED FENNEL SEEDS
1 TABLESPOON CHOPPED FENNEL GREENS
$1^1/_2$ TEASPOONS GRATED LEMON ZEST
2 TABLESPOONS CHOPPED FRESH FLAT-LEAF PARSLEY
$1/_2$ CUP (2 OZ/60G) FRESH BREAD CRUMBS
$1^1/_2$ CUPS PLUS 2 TABLESPOONS (13 FL OZ/390ML) BEEF OR
   CHICKEN STOCK
SALT AND FRESHLY GROUND BLACK PEPPER
2 RED BELL PEPPERS, CORED, SEEDED, AND CUT INTO $1^1/_2$-INCH STRIPS
2 MEDIUM FENNEL BULBS, TRIMMED, QUARTERED FROM TOP TO BOTTOM
$1/_2$ TEASPOON CHOPPED FRESH THYME
THYME SPRIGS AS A GARNISH

Cut each steak horizontally in half almost all the way to the other side so it opens like a book. Flatten slightly with a meat mallet.

Cut the carrot, onion, celery, and small fennel bulb into $1/8$-inch (0.3-cm) dice. Warm 2 tablespoons of the olive oil in a large skillet over medium heat. Add the vegetables and cook until soft, 12 to 15 minutes. Add the garlic and continue to cook for 1 minute. Remove from the pan and place in a bowl with $1/2$ teaspoon of the fennel seeds, fennel greens, 1 teaspoon of the lemon zest, the parsley, and bread crumbs. Add 2 table-spoons beef stock and mix together just until moistened. Season to taste with salt and pepper. Place the mixture on the beef and spread evenly. Roll the beef and tie with kitchen string at 1-inch intervals.

Warm 1 tablespoon olive oil in a skillet over medium-high heat. Brown the meat on all sides, turning occasionally, about 10 minutes. Add the remaining 1 1/2 cups (12 fl oz/360ml) beef stock, reduce the heat to low, cover, and simmer until the internal temperature is 130°F (54°C), 35 to 45 minutes.

In the meantime, bring a saucepan of salted water to a boil. Add the fennel and simmer until crisp, yet almost tender, 4 to 5 minutes. Let cool. Preheat the broiler and adjust the shelf so that it is 4 to 5 inches from the heat source.

In a bowl, toss together the peppers, fennel, remaining 1 tablespoon olive oil, and salt and pepper to taste. In a single layer, place the peppers and fennel on a baking sheet and broil for 4 to 5 minutes. Turn and continue to broil until they are golden and tender, 3 to 5 minutes. Remove from the oven and place in a bowl with the thyme, remaining 1/4 teaspoon fennel seed, and 1/2 teaspoon lemon zest.

Remove the strings from the beef and carve the roast into 1/4- to 1/2-inch (0.6- to 1.25-cm) slices. Reduce the pan juices by one-quarter. Place the beef on a platter and drizzle with the pan juices. Place the peppers and fennel around the edges and garnish with thyme sprigs. Serve immediately.

SERVES 6

From the

I've always thought of orchards

as safe havens. When I was a kid, I used to spend long afternoons playing hide-and-seek with my cousins among the apple, peach, and pear trees on my grandparents' farm. The shady canopy of branches, the orderly rows of trees, the soft carpet of leaves in the fall, and the sweet perfume of the ripening fruit made us feel sheltered and cozy in our private world.

I still feel that way. Sometimes, when I'm driving around in the California countryside and I see a beautiful orchard, I'll suddenly decide to pull over, walk under the trees, and just sit and think. There's just something wonderfully reassuring about being surrounded by all those branches offering up their sweet treasures.

California is such a paradise of orchards! In just an hour's drive from the heart of San Francisco, I can be face to face with some of the finest tree fruit imaginable. There are juicy Santa Rosa plums and cherries from the Suisun Valley. Peaches, nectarines, and plums grow to the south, apples, pears and quince to the north.

And about an hour northeast, in Brentwood, is the idyllic Frog Hollow Farms, where Al Courchesne

("Farmer Al" to his friends) and Becky Smith grow some really incredible organic fruit. They've got peaches, nectarines, cherries, apricots, plums, Asian and European pears, and even pluots (a cross between a plum and an apricot that somehow captures the best of both). When Al first started farming, he didn't know that he was supposed to pick the fruit green for storage and shipping. He picked it when it was perfectly ripe and sweet, and he's never changed his timing. His "misguided" thinking helped him build a reputation for producing some of the tastiest fruit in the Bay Area—all grown with a deep commitment to organic farming and to sustainable agriculture practices that nurture the soil and protect the environment.

Last fall, I spent a day at another of my favorite orchards, a place that's simply called The Apple Farm. When the owners, Don and Sally Schmitt, sold their fabulously successful restaurant in the Napa Valley, their dream was to move north and start a family farm. And when they discovered a wonderful old apple orchard in a storybook setting in Philo, in the idyllic Anderson Valley, they knew they'd found what they were looking for.

Orchard

ORCHARD

Apple season at the Apple Farm, Philo, California.
Opposite: Joanne enjoys freshly harvested produce.

Today, three generations of the family live and work on the farm. The Schmitts have made it their mission to track down and cultivate heirloom apples—what Don Schmitt calls "the old, traditional ones that still taste good." From an original thirteen varieties that were growing in the orchard when they took it over, the Schmitts have grafted in more than sixty.

Visitors can sample whatever's in season, browsing among the bushel baskets that display the year of each variety's origin. Don grabbed a buck knife and began slicing off hunks for me to try. I was amazed at how completely different they all tasted, and I fell in love with their charm-

ing names. The Winter Banana is a crisp, pale apple that's perfect for salads. One taste and my mind went straight to Gorgonzola or blue cheese with toasted pecans and lettuce in a sherry vinaigrette. The Northern Spy is a sweet, versatile fruit that's great for cooking or eating. The Splendour, originally from New Zealand, dates back to 1948. And the Swaar—dense and firm, perfect for eating with a slab of sharp Cheddar—is what Don calls a "good keeper," because it's quite tart when it's harvested, but when you store it in a cool cellar, its flavor gets better and better. (Speaking of storing, the Schmitts recommend keeping apples in the refrigerator to preserve their flavor and texture. I agree.)

As I toured the orchard with the Schmitts'

daughter, Karen, she told me about how the family had recognized early on that to be successful they would need to do more than just grow great apples. With their love of fine food and their restaurant background, they soon turned their hands to creating all kinds of wonderful apple products.

Nothing is wasted: The twigs are bundled and sold as kindling, while the less-than-picture-perfect apples go straight to the cider shed. Karen's husband, Tim, runs the cider press, and he showed me how the apples are ground into a pulp, which is spread into burlap-lined frames. The frames are stacked and pressed by hand.

Tim held out a paper cup to catch the first pressing as it flowed through the cloth and handed me the sweetest, freshest apple cider I've ever tasted. Some of the cider is fermented to make hard cider, some is made into vinegar, and some is boiled down to make old-fashioned apple syrup. And that's just for starters. The Schmitts also make chutneys, jellies, jams, dried apples, and even dried apple wreaths for the holidays.

People like the Al Courchesne, Becky Smith, and the Schmitt family really inspire me. They're living proof that small farming still has a place in our big, complicated world. But they're more than just farmers. They've devoted their lives to restoring and preserving what's best in nature. And by doing that, they've made their orchards into safe havens for all of us.

Different varieties of apples have markedly different flavors.

Olive Oil and Orange-Essence Cake with Soft Cream

5 EGGS, SEPARATED

$3/_4$ CUP (5 OZ/150G) SUGAR

2 TABLESPOONS GRATED ORANGE ZEST

$1/_3$ CUP (4 FL OZ/120ML) EXTRA-VIRGIN OLIVE OIL

$1/_3$ CUP ($2^1/_2$ FL OZ/80ML) SWEET MUSCAT, LATE-HARVEST RIESLING, OR GEWÜRZTRAMINER WINE

$2^1/_2$ TABLESPOONS ($1^1/_4$ FL OZ/40ML) ORANGE-FLOWER WATER

1 CUP ($3^1/_2$ OZ/100G) SIFTED ALL-PURPOSE FLOUR

$1/_4$ TEASPOON SALT

$1/_2$ TEASPOON CREAM OF TARTAR

1 CUP (8 FL OZ/240ML) HEAVY CREAM

3 TABLESPOONS (1 OZ/30G) CONFECTIONERS' SUGAR

$1/_4$ TEASPOON VANILLA EXTRACT

Butter and flour a 9-inch (23-cm) springform pan or line the bottom with baking parchment. Preheat the oven to 350°F (175°C).

Separate the eggs and beat the yolks with half the sugar until well ribboned. Beat in the orange zest, slowly whisk in the olive oil, drop by drop, and finally add the wine and orange-flower water. Mix together the flour and salt and beat the dry ingredients into the egg mixture.

Beat the egg whites with the cream of tartar until they hold soft peaks. Beat in the remaining sugar until the whites hold stiff peaks. Fold the whites into the batter. Pour into the prepared pan and bake for 20 minutes. Lower the oven temperature to 300°F (150°C) continue to bake another 20 minutes. Turn off the oven, cover the top of the cake with a round of buttered baking parchment, and leave in the oven for another 10 minutes. Remove from the oven and let cool in the pan on a rack.

To serve, whip the cream to soft peaks and add 1 tablespoon confectioners' sugar and the vanilla. Slice the cake and serve a wedge of the cake with the cream on the side. Dust the top with the remaining 2 tablespoons confectioners' sugar.

SERVES 8 TO 10

I wouldn't use a bottle of Château d'Yquem, the most expensive Sauternes in the world, for this recipe. I would probably choose a late-harvest Riesling, Muscat, or Gewürztraminer. Same principle as Yquem. If you leave the grapes on the vine for that much longer, the grapes lose some of their water through evaporation, which in effect concentrates the sugar. After Botrytis cinerea, or noble rot, invades the grape and the grapes are pressed, you get amber-gold wines with hints of orange blossom and honeysuckle. Late-harvest wines are perfect for serving with dessert, but also they add sweetness and flavor to this light and airy cake.

Summer Melons in Sweet Spiced Wine

1 ORANGE

1¹/₂ CUPS (12 FL OZ/350ML) LATE-HARVEST DESSERT WINE,
  SUCH AS REISLING, GEWÜRZTRAMINER, MUSCAT, OR SAUTERNES

1 TABLESPOON HONEY

¹/₂ VANILLA BEAN, SPLIT AND SCRAPED

4 ¹/₄-INCH (0.6-CM) SLICES FRESH GINGER

5 POUNDS (4.5KG) ASSORTED MELONS, CANTALOUPE, HONEYDEW,
  CRENSHAW, CASABA, OR PERSIAN

A late-harvest wine means that the grapes have been allowed to stay on the vine after the regular harvest, developing a beneficial mold called botrytis. As the fruit withers on the vine, the juice concentrates with greater sweetness, a perfect match for dessert. In this recipe, I have made a syrup to be used as a sauce for the melons. Chilled and served on a warm summer evening under the stars, this simple dessert is so refreshing.

Peel the orange with a vegetable peeler, making sure there is no white pith on the back. Juice the orange. Bring the orange juice, orange peel, wine, honey, vanilla bean, and ginger root to a boil in a saucepan over high heat. Reduce the heat to low and simmer for 5 minutes. Remove from the heat and remove the orange peel, vanilla bean, and ginger root and discard. Let cool for 30 minutes.

In the meantime, using a melon baller, form balls of melon and place in a large glass bowl. Pour the orange-infused wine over the melon and let sit in the refrigerator for 1 hour, until the melon is chilled.

To serve, ladle the melon into bowls and pour the sauce over the melon.

SERVES 6

Raspberry and Zinfandel Sherbet
with Warm Berry Compote

I like nothing better after a big lunch or dinner than to have a bowl of homemade ice cream or fresh fruit sherbet. Imagine frosted glasses filled with icy cold Zinfandel and raspberry sherbet, topped with a warm compote of raspberries and blueberries, on a blazing hot day in the middle of summer. Refreshing to say the least!

FOR THE SHERBET

3 CUPS (24 FL OZ/725ML) FRUITY ZINFANDEL
1 CUP PLUS 2 TABLESPOONS ($7^1/_2$ OZ/220G) SUGAR
6 CUPS (24 OZ/700G) RASPBERRIES

FOR THE COMPOTE

2 CUPS (8 OZ/240G) RASPBERRIES
$^1/_3$ CUP ($2^1/_2$ OZ/75G) SUGAR
1 PIECE OF LEMON PEEL, 2 INCHES (5CM) LONG, REMOVED WITH
   A VEGETABLE PEELER
$^3/_4$ CUP (3 OZ/90G) BLUEBERRIES
$^3/_4$ CUP (3 OZ/90G) FRAISES DES BOIS OR WILD STRAWBERRIES (OPTIONAL)
1 TABLESPOON CRÈME DE CASSIS
1 TEASPOON LEMON JUICE

For the sherbet, heat the Zinfandel, sugar, and $^1/_3$ cup ($2^1/_2$ fl oz/80 ml) water to a boil. As soon as it comes to a boil, pour it over the raspberries. Let steep 30 minutes.

For the compote, puree 1 cup (4 oz/120 g) of the raspberries in a food processor or blender to obtain a smooth puree. Strain through a fine mesh strainer into a clean bowl. Place $^1/_2$ cup (4 fl oz/120 ml) water, the sugar, and lemon peel in a medium pan over medium high heat and bring to a boil. Reduce the heat to medium and add the blueberries. Cook until the blueberries just begin to crack, about 1 minute. Add the fraises des bois. Remove the lemon peel and discard. Stir in the raspberry puree, crème de cassis, and remaining 1 cup (4 oz/120 g) raspberries. You should have 2 cups.

Puree the raspberry and Zinfandel mixture in a blender and strain through a fine strainer. Refrigerate the mixture until well chilled. Freeze according to the directions for your ice cream maker.

To serve, place the compote in a saucepan over medium heat and warm for about 1 minute. Scoop the sherbet into bowls and spoon the warm compote over the top. Serve immediately.

SERVES 6

Apricot Upside-Down Cake

12 TABLESPOONS (6 OZ/180G) UNSALTED BUTTER

$^3/_4$ CUP (6 OZ/180G) BROWN SUGAR

1 POUND (450G) FRESH APRICOTS, HALVED AND PITTED

$1^1/_2$ CUPS (6 OZ/180G) ALL-PURPOSE FLOUR

2 TEASPOONS BAKING POWDER

$^1/_4$ TEASPOON SALT

1 CUP (7 OZ/210G) SUGAR

2 EGGS

$1^1/_4$ TEASPOONS VANILLA EXTRACT

$^1/_2$ CUP (4 FL OZ/120ML) WHOLE MILK

PINCH OF CREAM OF TARTAR

1 CUP (8 FL OZ/240ML) HEAVY CREAM

1 TABLESPOON CONFECTIONERS' SUGAR

*T*his summertime cake is inspired by Lindsey Shere, pastry chef at Chez Panisse Restaurant, where I worked for several years. Lindsey has a knack for making desserts just like my mother and grand-mother—real comfort foods I come back to again and again!

Butter a 9-inch (23-cm) cake pan. Place the pan over medium heat and melt 4 tablespoons of the butter and brown sugar in the bottom of the pan. Place the apricot halves on top of the melted butter and brown sugar, skin side down.

Preheat the oven to 350°F (175°C). For the cake, sift the flour, baking powder, and salt together. Cream the remaining 8 tablespoons (4 oz/120g) butter and sugar together in a bowl until light. Separate the eggs and add the yolks, one at a time, beating well after each addition. Add 1 teaspoon of the vanilla and mix well. Add the milk and the dry ingredients alternately to the batter, folding well after each addition. Beat the egg whites to form soft peaks. Add the cream of tartar and continue to beat until stiff peaks form. Fold the whites into the cake batter. Spread the batter over the apricots and bake until a skewer inserted into the center comes out clean, 55 to 60 minutes.

Cool the cake for 10 to 15 minutes and run a knife around the edges of the pan to loosen it. Turn the cake over onto a serving platter and let it sit another 5 minutes. Remove the pan.

To serve, whip the heavy cream until soft peaks are formed. Sift the confectioners' sugar on top of the cream, add the remaining $^1/_4$ teaspoon vanilla, and fold together. Serve with the cake.

SERVES 8 TO 10

Fresh Cherries with Cassis Zabaglione

4 EGG YOLKS
$^1/_4$ CUP (1$^1/_2$ OZ/50G) SUGAR
6 TABLESPOONS (3 FL OZ/90ML) CRÈME DE CASSIS
2 POUNDS (1.8KG) CHERRIES, PITTED

Have a saucepan of barely simmering water ready 15 minutes before serving. Whisk the egg yolks, sugar, and 2 tablespoons water together in a large bowl. Whisk in the crème de cassis and set the bowl over the pan of barely simmering water. Don't let the water touch the bottom of the bowl. Whisk constantly until the mixture is thick, frothy, begins to hold soft peaks, and there is no liquid left at the bottom of the bowl, 5 to 8 minutes.

To serve, divide the cherries among 6 large wine glasses. Spoon the zabaglione onto the cherries and serve immediately.

SERVES 6

In May, when cherries come into season, I'm always thrilled. Try matching them up with zabaglione, one of Italy's great desserts. This ethereal foamy custard sauce is made with egg yolks, sugar, and usually Marsala. I've substituted crème de cassis for the Marsala, a nice match for the cherries.

Unlimited Crisp Recipes

I HAVE NEVER BEEN ONE for rich, sweet, gooey desserts. When I am in the mood for one, just a single bite of chocolate will do the trick. But for the most part, you will see me heading towards the fruit on any menu or at the farmer's market.

One thing still remains true for me, my all-time favorite dessert is a crisp. You can use the recipe on page 172, but here are some additional ideas for the fruit:

*   *   *

Peeled and sliced apples
Peeled and sliced apples and raisins
Peeled and sliced apples and dried cranberries
Peeled and sliced pears and apples

Peeled and sliced pears and dried fruits
Peeled and sliced pears and ginger
Peeled and sliced peaches and blueberries
Peeled and sliced peaches and plums

Sliced nectarines and blackberries
Sliced nectarines and raspberries
Mixed berries
Halved figs and raspberries
Strawberries and rhubarb
Apricots and raspberries
Cherries and apricots

Peach and Blueberry Crisp

Hot-from-the-oven crisp with vanilla ice cream on the side can't be beat. Peaches might very well be my favorite fruit, but for this recipe, they need to be peeled. Sometimes when I am feeling lazy or strapped for time, I will substitute nectarines. Remember that this topping is versatile—use whatever fresh, seasonal fruit is available. When you're making the topping, double or triple it. Use what you need and freeze the rest. Then whenever you want to make a crisp, cut up the fruit, toss with sugar, place in a baking dish, and top with the frozen topping. Simple!

FOR THE CRISP TOPPING
3/4 CUP (3 1/2 OZ/100G) PECANS OR WALNUTS, TOASTED (SEE PAGE 78)
1 1/2 CUPS (6 OZ/180G) ALL-PURPOSE FLOUR
1/2 CUP (4 OZ/120G) BROWN SUGAR
1/4 TEASPOON FRESHLY GRATED NUTMEG
8 TABLESPOONS (4 OZ/120G) UNSALTED BUTTER, AT ROOM TEMPERATURE

FOR THE FRUIT FILLING
3 POUNDS (1.4KG) PEACHES
2 CUPS (8 OZ/240G) BLUEBERRIES
3 TABLESPOONS (1 OZ/30G) ALL-PURPOSE FLOUR
2 TABLESPOONS SUGAR

Place the nuts in the food processor and pulse a few times until the nuts are in 1/4-inch (0.6-cm) pieces. Remove the nuts and reserve. In a bowl, mix together the flour, brown sugar, and nutmeg. Add the dry ingredients and butter to the food processor and pulse until it just begins to hold together. Add the nuts and pulse 3 to 4 more times until mixed.

Preheat the oven to 375°F (190°C).

To peel the peaches, you can either use a knife or bring a large saucepan of water to a boil. Boil the peaches for 20 seconds. Remove and cool enough to handle. Peel the peaches and cut them into 3/4-inch (2-cm) wedges. Discard the pits.

In a bowl, toss together the peaches, blueberries, flour, and sugar until well mixed. Place the fruit in a 2 to 2 1/2 quart (2 to 2.2L) baking dish and sprinkle the crisp topping evenly over the top. Bake in the middle of the oven until a skewer inserted into the center goes in without any resistance, the top is golden, and the fruit mixture is bubbling around the edges, 35 to 40 minutes. Remove from the oven and let cool for 20 minutes before serving.

To serve, spoon the crisp into individual dessert dishes.

SERVES 8

Cornmeal Cake
with Cinnamon-Poached Pears

FOR THE PEARS
2 CUPS (16 FL OZ/475ML) PORT
6 CINNAMON STICKS
12 WHOLE CLOVES, TIED TOGETHER IN CHEESECLOTH
1 CUP (6¹/₂ OZ/200G) SUGAR
6 MEDIUM BOSC PEARS, PEELED, QUARTERED, AND CORED

CAKE
4 CUPS (32 FL OZ/900ML) WHOLE MILK
¹/₂ CUP PLUS 1 TABLESPOON (4 OZ/120G) SUGAR
1 CUP (5 OZ/150G) FINE CORNMEAL
1 EGG
4 EGG YOLKS
4 TABLESPOONS (2 OZ/60G) UNSALTED BUTTER, AT ROOM TEMPERATURE
GRATED ZEST OF 1 LARGE ORANGE
CONFECTIONERS' SUGAR

This is a favorite harvest or winter dessert. If possible, warm the pears in their syrup just before serving. As an added note, a dollop of softly whipped cream sweetened with confectioners' sugar and flavored with vanilla extract will only make the dish even more delicious.

In a saucepan over medium heat, bring the port and 2 cups (16 fl oz/475ml) of water to a boil, and add the cinnamon sticks, cloves, and sugar. Add the pears and simmer until they are tender and can be easily pierced with a fork, 20 to 30 minutes. Discard the cloves and reserve the pears. Reduce the poaching liquid by half and reserve.

Place the milk and sugar in a saucepan over medium-high heat and bring to a boil. Gradually add the cornmeal, whisking constantly. Simmer until it is very thick, about 25 minutes. Let cool to lukewarm. Stir in the whole egg, egg yolks, butter, and orange zest.

Preheat the oven to 375°F (190°C). Butter a 9-inch (23-cm) cake pan. Spread the polenta in the pan and bake until it just begins to turn golden and firm to the touch in the center, 30 to 35 minutes. Turn out on a cooling rack and let cool for 15 minutes.

To serve, cut the cake into wedges and place on individual plates. Spoon pears, cinnamon sticks, and reduced poaching liquid around each piece of cake, dust with confectioners' sugar, and serve.

SERVES 8

Warm Nectarine and Polenta Tart with Soft Cream

2 POUNDS (1.8KG) MEDIUM-RIPE NECTARINES, PITTED AND
    CUT INTO $^1/_4$-INCH (0.6-CM) SLICES
2 TABLESPOONS ALL-PURPOSE FLOUR
$^1/_3$ CUP ($2^1/_2$ OZ/70G) SUGAR
$^1/_4$ TEASPOON FRESHLY GRATED NUTMEG

DOUGH
11 TABLESPOONS ($5^1/_2$ OZ/165G) UNSALTED BUTTER,
    AT ROOM TEMPERATURE
$^3/_4$ CUP (5 OZ/150G) SUGAR
3 EGG YOLKS
$1^3/_4$ CUPS (7 OZ/210G) ALL-PURPOSE FLOUR
$^1/_2$ CUP ($3^1/_2$ OZ/75G) POLENTA
PINCH OF SALT
1 CUP (8 FL OZ/240ML) HEAVY CREAM
2 TABLESPOONS CONFECTIONERS' SUGAR
$^1/_4$ TEASPOON VANILLA EXTRACT

When summer comes, I always look forward to stone fruits such as nectarines, apricots, peaches, and plums. I have the best memories of my grandfather's orchard. He would pick the fruit as my grandmother and mother would simmer big batches of jams and jellies and bake all kinds of pies and tarts. I don't think my grandmother or my mother would have considered putting polenta into a pastry back then, but I can guarantee they would have loved the crunchy results as much as I do.

In a bowl, toss the nectarines with the flour, $^1/_3$ cup sugar, and the nutmeg. Reserve.

For the dough, cream the butter and sugar in a food processor until well blended, about 1 minute. Add the egg yolks, one at a time, pulsing after each addition. Sift together the flour, polenta, and salt and mix into the creamed mixture. Mix until the dough comes together. Cut the dough in half and return half to the refrigerator. Press the remaining dough evenly into the bottom and sides of an $8^1/_2$-inch (21-cm) tart pan. Spoon the nectarines into the tart shell evenly.

Preheat the oven to 375°F (190°C). Roll out the remaining dough into a $^1/_4$-inch (0.6-cm) thick piece. With a shaped cookie cutter, such as a heart, cut as many shapes as you possibly can from the rolled polenta dough. Place them on top of the nectarines, placing the top of the heart shapes around the edges in concentric circles, overlapping slightly. Bake until golden, 35 to 40 minutes. Cool on a rack and serve warm, if possible.

To serve, whip the heavy cream until soft peaks are formed. Sift the confectioners' sugar on top of the cream, add the vanilla and fold together. Serve with the tart.

SERVES 8

Lemon Cloud Tart

For the Pastry

1¼ cups (5 oz/150g) all-purpose flour

1 tablespoon sugar

Pinch of salt

1 teaspoon grated lemon zest

10 tablespoons (5 oz/150g) unsalted butter, removed from
the refrigerator for 15 minutes, cut into small pieces

For the Filling

4 egg yolks

⅓ cup (2½ oz/75g) sugar

⅓ cup (2½ fl oz/80ml) lemon juice

3 tablespoons (1 oz/30g) grated lemon zest

3 tablespoons (1½ oz/45g) unsalted butter, melted

⅓ cup (1½ oz/45g) blanched almonds, toasted and ground

For the Meringue

3 egg whites, at room temperature

¾ cup (5 oz/150g) sugar

½ teaspoon vanilla extract

Lemon, lemon, lemon! This recipe is inspired from my "Seasonal Celebrations" series of cookbooks—Spring, Summer, Autumn, and Winter. I include it here because its flavors sing with lemon and the crust and meringue melt in your mouth.

When our grandmothers were kids, lemon meringue pie—an American classic—was made in the spring, when eggs and lemons are abundant. The flavors burst with lemon. Now it's a year-round favorite.

In the food processor fitted with the metal blade, mix the flour, sugar, and salt with a few pulses. Add the lemon zest and butter and pulse until the mixture resembles cornmeal. Add as much water as needed until the pastry just holds together in a ball, up to 1 tablespoon. Remove from the processor, flatten into a 6-inch (15-cm) cake, and wrap it in plastic. Refrigerate for 30 minutes.

Preheat the oven to 400°F (200°C). Press the pastry evenly into the bottom and sides of a 9-inch (23-cm) tart pan. Set the tart shell in the freezer for 30 minutes.

Line the pastry with baking parchment and scatter 1 cup (7 oz/210g) of dry beans or pie weights over the parchment. Bake the tart shell until the top edges are light golden, 10 to 15 minutes. Remove the parchment and weights, reduce the heat to 375°F (190°C), and continue to bake until the shell is light golden, 15 to 20 minutes more.

While the tart shell is baking, beat the egg yolks and sugar until they form a stiff ribbon. Stir in the lemon juice and grated zest, then the melted butter and almonds. Pour the filling into the prebaked shell and bake until a skewer inserted into the center comes out clean, 20 to 30 minutes. Remove the tart from the oven and let cool completely.

To finish the tart, preheat the oven to 450°F (230°C). Place the egg whites in a bowl and, with an electric mixer, beat them until they form soft peaks. Add the sugar, a little at a time, and continue beating until they form stiff peaks. Fold in the vanilla. Spread the meringue on top of the filling, making peaks. Bake the tart in the middle of the oven until the meringue is golden brown, about 7 minutes. Chill the tart until set, about 1 hour.

SERVES 8

Pears and Figs with Pecorino, Walnuts, and Honey

$^1/_2$ CUP (2$^1/_2$ OZ/75G) FRESH NEW CROP WALNUTS
1 CHUNK PECORINO, ABOUT 6 OUNCES (180G)
1 RIPE RED BARTLETT PEAR
2 RIPE GREEN BARTLETT PEARS
12 RIPE FIGS, AN ASSORTMENT IF AVAILABLE
3 TABLESPOONS 1$^1/_2$ FL OZ/45ML) CHESTNUT HONEY,
    OR OTHER FLAVORFUL HONEY
6 FIG LEAVES AS A GARNISH

Preheat the oven to 350°F (175°C).

Place the walnuts on a baking sheet and bake until light golden, 5 to 7 minutes.

Shave several pieces of the pecorino using three-quarters of the cheese. Halve the pears and core them. Cut the pear halves each into 3 wedges. Halve the figs.

To serve, place the fig leaves on a large platter. Top with the pears. Disperse the figs, some with the cut-side up and some with the cut-side down, between the pears. Top with the shaved pecorino. Warm the honey in a saucepan over low heat, 1 minute. Drizzle the honey over the top. Scatter the walnut halves onto the top before serving.

SERVES 6

Spanish friars who traveled from Mexico north through California not only built the lovely mission churches but they also brought with them their beloved fig and planted it all over California. The dark purple fig with a rose center is called mission, in their honor. Other figs—the fat white-fleshed, green-skinned variety called Calimyrna and the small, thick-skinned, green fig, the Kadota, or an assortment—can also be used in this recipe. This is a terrific dessert served with a glass of port on a chilly autumn night.

Creamy Summer Berry and Lemon Gratin

4 LEMONS

1 1/2 CUPS (12 FL OZ/360ML) WHOLE MILK

5 EGG YOLKS

1 TEASPOON CORNSTARCH

1/3 CUP (2 1/2 OZ/75G) SUGAR

2 TABLESPOONS ALL-PURPOSE FLOUR

1/2 TEASPOON VANILLA EXTRACT

1 TABLESPOON LEMON JUICE

1 TABLESPOON UNSALTED BUTTER, AT ROOM TEMPERATURE

1/2 CUP (4 OZ/120G) MASCARPONE

4 CUPS (16 OZ/480G) MIXED BERRIES, BLUEBERRIES, BLACKBERRIES,
    RASPBERRIES, BOYSENBERRIES

2 TABLESPOONS CONFECTIONERS' SUGAR

Every time I teach this dessert in class, I have students almost licking their plates. It's creamy, not too sweet, lemony, and comforting—everything a dessert should be. It can also be made with peaches or nectarines, and in the winter, you can make it with blood or navel orange sections.

Peel the lemons with a vegetable peeler avoiding the white pith. Scald the milk in a saucepan over medium heat. Add the lemon peel and remove from the heat. Let sit for 1 hour. After 1 hour, strain the milk to remove the lemon peel and discard the peel.

In a bowl, beat the egg yolks until light and fluffy. In another bowl, combine the cornstarch, sugar, and flour. Add this mixture to the egg yolks and beat until light and fluffy, about 1 minute.

Scald the milk a second time and add the warm milk slowly to the eggs, whisking constantly. Place the mixture back in the saucepan and over low heat, stirring, cook until the mixture thickens and bubbles around the edges. Remove from the heat and whisk in the vanilla, lemon juice, and butter. Fold in the mascarpone until well mixed.

Preheat the broiler.

Divide the custard mixture among 6 or 8 individual gratin or tartlet dishes, 5 inches (13cm) in diameter. Press the berries into the custard mixture. Sift the confectioners' sugar over the top. Broil until the tops are golden brown, 1 to 2 minutes. Serve hot or at room temperature.

SERVES 6 TO 8

Tangerine Ice Cream with a Citrus Compote

7 TANGERINES
2 CUPS (16 FL OZ/475ML) MILK
2 CUPS (16 FL OZ/475ML) HEAVY CREAM
$^3/_4$ CUP (5 OZ/150G) SUGAR
8 EGG YOLKS
3 TABLESPOONS (1$^1/_2$ FL OZ/45ML) TANGERINE JUICE
2 TABLESPOONS GRAND MARNIER
$^1/_4$ TEASPOON VANILLA EXTRACT

FOR THE COMPOTE
1$^1/_4$ CUPS (10 FL OZ/300ML) TANGERINE JUICE
2 TABLESPOONS HONEY
$^1/_4$ CUP (1$^1/_2$ OZ/45G) GOLDEN RAISINS
6 KUMQUATS, THINLY SLICED AND SEEDS REMOVED
2 KIWI FRUIT, PEELED AND COARSELY DICED
3 BLOOD ORANGES, PEELED AND SECTIONED (OPTIONAL)
2 PASSION FRUIT, SEEDS ONLY (OPTIONAL)
6 STRAWBERRIES, SLICED

When I was a kid, my grandfather would spread a long, white tablecloth under the maple trees at his farm. He would make us the grandest lunch, finished off with ice cream we had churned with the old hand-crank machine stored in the back pantry. But ice cream wasn't just a summer treat; we enjoyed it year-round. Here is a winter version, flavored with citrus.

Remove the zest from 2 tangerines and reserve. Squeeze enough tangerine juice to make 3 tablespoons (1$^1/_2$ fl oz/45ml) and reserve separately. Remove the peel of the remaining 5 tangerines with a vegetable peeler. In a large saucepan, combine the milk, heavy cream, sugar, and tangerine peel and stir well. Scald and turn off the heat. Let stand for 2 hours.

In another saucepan, whisk the egg yolks in a bowl for 5 seconds to break them up. Scald the cream mixture again. Add the cream mixture to the yolks, drop by drop, whisking constantly. Turn on the heat to medium. Stirring constantly, bring the mixture to 170°F (76°C), or just until it begins to thicken and coats the back of a wooden spoon. Whisk for 30 seconds to cool the mixture and strain immediately into a bowl. Add the reserved tangerine zest and tangerine juice, the Grand Marnier, and vanilla extract. Refrigerate the mixture until well chilled. Freeze according to the instructions with your ice cream maker.

For the citrus compote, combine the tangerine juice, honey, raisins, and kumquats in a saucepan over medium-high heat and stir well. Heat the mixture just until it boils for about 30 seconds. Let it cool.

To serve, scoop the ice cream into bowls. Spoon the compote over the ice cream and garnish with kiwi fruit, blood oranges, passion fruit seeds, and sliced strawberries, distributing evenly. Serve immediately.

MAKES ABOUT 1$^1/_2$ QUARTS (1.4L) AND SERVES 6

Baked Apples
Filled with Dried Fruits and Nuts

6 APPLES, DELICIOUS, CORTLAND, ROME BEAUTY, OR MCINTOSH
$^1/_2$ CUP (4 OZ/120G) BROWN SUGAR
5 TABLESPOONS (2$^1/_2$ OZ/75G) UNSALTED BUTTER, MELTED
$^3/_4$ TEASPOON CINNAMON
$^3/_4$ TEASPOON GRATED LEMON ZEST
$^1/_4$ CUP (1 OZ/30G) WALNUTS, TOASTED (PAGE 78) AND COARSELY CHOPPED
$^1/_4$ CUP (1 OZ/30G) DRIED APPLES, CHOPPED
$^1/_4$ CUP (1 OZ/30G) GOLDEN RAISINS
$^1/_4$ CUP (1 OZ/30G) DRIED APRICOTS, CHOPPED
4 AMARETTI COOKIES, CRUSHED
$^3/_4$ CUP (6 FL OZ/180ML) MASCARPONE

Preheat the oven to 375°F (190°C). Core the apples, cutting to within $^1/_2$ inch (1.25 cm) of the bottom, but leaving the bottom intact. Cut a slice $^1/_2$ inch (1.25 cm) thick off the stem end and set aside.

In a small pan over medium-high heat, combine 6 tablespoons (3 oz/90g) of the brown sugar, 3 tablespoons (1$^1/_2$ oz/45g) butter, $^3/_4$ cup (6 fl oz/180ml) water, $^1/_2$ teaspoon of the cinnamon, and the lemon zest. Bring to a boil, stirring to dissolve the sugar. Remove the syrup from the heat and set aside.

In a bowl, mix together the walnuts, dried apples, raisins, apricots, the remaining 2 tablespoons (1 oz/30g) brown sugar, remaining $^1/_4$ teaspoon cinnamon, remaining 2 tablespoons (1 oz/30g) melted butter, and three-quarters of the crushed amaretti. Reserve the remaining crushed amaretti. Fill the apples with the mixture, distributing evenly. Place the top of the apple back on top of the filling.

Place the apples in a 2-quart (2 L) baking dish and pour the syrup over them. Cover with foil, place in the oven, and cook until the apples are tender, about 30 minutes. Baste with the pan juices and continue to cook, the apples covered with aluminum foil, until the apples are just tender, 10 to 15 minutes, depending upon the variety of the apple.

When the apples are done, remove the foil and spoon some of the syrup over the top.

To serve, spoon the mascarpone into the hole on the top of each hot baked apple, distributing evenly. Sprinkle the mascarpone with the reserved crushed amaretti. Drizzle the syrup from the pan around the edges before serving.

SERVES 6

*A*utumn—when the summer heat finally relaxes and gives way to cool, clear days and chilly nights, is the time for harvesting grapes and picking pears, walnuts, and apples as the bounty of the vineyard and orchard is upon us. Top these sweet baked stuffed apples with a dollop of mascarpone when they are hot from the oven, and watch it melt down the sides.

Lavender and Toasted Almond Ice Cream with Warm Baked Figs

5 TABLESPOONS (2 OZ/60G) SUGAR

2 TABLESPOONS DRIED LAVENDER FLOWERS

2 CUPS (16 FL OZ/475ML) WHOLE MILK

2 CUPS (16 FL OZ/475ML) HEAVY CREAM

1/2 CUP PLUS 2 TABLESPOONS (5 FL OZ/150ML) HONEY, PREFERABLY
LAVENDER HONEY

8 EGG YOLKS

3/4 CUP (3 OZ/90G) ALMONDS, TOASTED AND CHOPPED

15 RIPE FIGS

2 TABLESPOONS PORT

In the Wine Country, I have a few pots of lavender. The scent always reminds me of my first trip to France, when I scurried to the market to buy little Provençal sachets or handmade soaps to bring home to all of my friends. I still love the scent. I either pick my own lavender flowers and dry them in the sun or buy dried lavender at the health food store. The most important thing is not to cook with any flowers that have been sprayed with chemicals. And use lavender honey in this recipe if you can find it.

In a small heavy saucepan over medium-high heat, combine the sugar, lavender, and 1 tablespoon water. Cook until the sugar dissolves and the mixture caramelizes, 2 to 3 minutes. Place on an oiled baking sheet and let cool. Grind in a spice grinder or clean coffee grinder to form a fine dust. Remove any large pieces and reserve. This can be made in advance and stored in an airtight container for up to a month.

In a large saucepan, scald the milk, heavy cream, and 1/2 cup (4 fl oz/ 125 ml) of the honey. In another saucepan, whisk together the egg yolks. After the milk mixture has scalded, add it to the yolks, drop by drop at first and tablespoon by tablespoon after a minute, whisking constantly. When all of the milk mixture has been added to the yolks, add the reserved lavender powder and stir well. Place the pan over low heat and stir constantly until the mixture lightly coats the back of a wooden spoon and the temperature is 170°F (76°C). Remove from the heat immediately and strain into a bowl. Whisk for 30 seconds to cool. Chill for several hours in the refrigerator.

Freeze the ice cream according to the directions for your ice cream maker. During the last 2 minutes, add the chopped almonds and mix thoroughly.

Preheat the oven to 350°F (175°C). Drizzle a 13- x 9-inch (33 x 23-cm) baking dish with the remaining 2 tablespoons honey. Halve the figs. Place the figs cut-side down in a baking dish and bake until the figs are tender, about 20 minutes. Turn the figs, add the port, and baste with the liquid in the pan. Return the figs to the oven for 5 minutes more.

To serve, scoop the ice cream into bowls and top with the warm figs and their sauce.

MAKES APPROXIMATELY 1 QUART (900ML) AND SERVES 10

Rustic Red and Green Plum Tart

FOR THE PASTRY
1 CUP (4 OZ/120G) ALL-PURPOSE FLOUR
$^1/_3$ CUP ($1^1/_4$ OZ/35G) CAKE FLOUR
$^1/_4$ TEASPOON SALT
12 TABLESPOONS (6 OZ/180G) UNSALTED BUTTER,
    CUT INTO $^1/_2$-INCH (1.25-CM) PIECES
2 TEASPOONS LEMON JUICE

FOR THE TOPPING
5 TO 6 MEDIUM YELLOW OR GREEN PLUMS, MEDIUM-RIPE,
    HALVED, PITTED AND CUT INTO THIN SLICES
5 TO 6 MEDIUM PURPLE OR RED PLUMS, MEDIUM-RIPE,
    HALVED, PITTED AND CUT INTO THIN SLICES
$^1/_4$ CUP ($1^1/_2$ OZ/50G) SUGAR
2 TABLESPOONS UNSALTED BUTTER, MELTED
$^1/_4$ CUP (2 OZ/60G) APRICOT JAM, MELTED AND STRAINED
1 CUP (8 FL OZ/240ML) HEAVY CREAM
2 TABLESPOONS CONFECTIONERS' SUGAR
$^1/_4$ TEASPOON VANILLA EXTRACT

This tart uses the simplest, most foolproof no-brainer puff pastry known to man. The results are fantastic. If you are pressed for time, substitute 3/4 pound (350g) prepared puff pastry. The dough can be stored in the refrigerator for up to 3 days and frozen for a couple of weeks. In the summer I use this dough with all kinds of fresh fruits, depending on what is in season. For plums, I suggest using greengage for the green variety and Santa Rosa for the red plums. If you happen to have a bottle of quetsch, the French plum brandy, add a few drops to the cream.

Mix the all-purpose flour, cake flour, and salt and place in freezer 1 hour before using. Place the butter in a bowl and also place it in the freezer 1 hour before using.

Transfer the cold flour mixture to the food processor. Add the butter and pulse several times until half of the butter is the size of peas and the remaining is smaller. Turn the contents onto a work surface, marble if possible. Make a well in the center. Combine the lemon juice and $^1/_3$ cup (3 fl oz/80ml) ice water and add to the cold flour and butter. Gather as best you can to make a ball. Press the dough together as best you can to form a rough rectangle shape, 4 x 6 inches (10 x 15cm). There will be large chunks of butter showing.

Roll out dough into a $^{1}/_{2}$-inch (1.25-cm) thick rectangle, 5 x 7 inches (13 x 20cm). Fold the narrow ends towards the center to meet in the center. Fold in half again so that there are 4 layers. Turn the dough a quarter of a turn and roll again to form a rectangle $^{1}/_{2}$-inch (1.25-cm) thick. This is your first turn. Repeat the folding process. This is your second turn. Repeat the rolling and turning process one more time. For the fourth turn, roll the dough and fold it into thirds as you would a business letter. Wrap the dough in plastic wrap and refrigerate for 45 to 60 minutes.

Preheat the oven to 400°F (200°C). Combine the plums and 3 tablespoons (1$^{1}/_{4}$ oz/40 g) of the sugar. Roll the pastry into a 12-inch (30-cm) circle and place on a baking sheet. Trim and crimp the edges. Sprinkle the dough with the remaining 1 tablespoon sugar. Place the plums in an overlapping decorative pattern in a single layer. Brush with melted butter and bake in the middle of the oven. After 10 minutes, reduce the heat to 375°F (190°C) and continue to bake for 25 to 35 minutes until golden and crisp. Remove from the oven and brush with jam. Let cool for 10 minutes.

To serve, whip the heavy cream until soft peaks are formed. Sift the confectioners' sugar on top of the cream, add the vanilla, and fold together. Serve with the tart.

MAKES 1 TART, 10 INCHES (25CM) IN DIAMETER, AND SERVES 6 TO 8

And Finally

My sweet tooth *must have fallen out when I was a kid, and it never grew back. I'm not one of those people who live for big, rich desserts. There's a restaurant in San Francisco that offers a one-bite serving of any of their desserts for a dollar. That's my kind of place. To me, there's no better way to end a meal than with a good, strong espresso and one really fabulous bite of something sweet—preferably something made with one or more of my dessert "holy trinity:" chocolate, lemon, and honey.*

After months of poking around in the fields, farms, and vineyards of Northern California doing research for this book, I decided it was time for a little coffee and dessert. So, for starters, I made a date to spend the day with Carlo di Ruocco, the man behind Mr. Espresso, a family-owned coffee roasting company in Oakland.

Walk into the warehouse and you're greeted—literally—by a hill of beans. Hundreds of bags from Costa Rica, Guatemala, Brazil, Colombia, Ethiopia, Kenya, and just about everywhere coffee is grown are stacked nearly two stories high. What makes Carlo's coffee really special is the masterful blending of these beans to achieve the right balance of flavors and fragrances. The art of roasting and blending is a lot like winemaking. It takes a discerning palate and years of experience to master.

The minute I walked into the roasting room, my heart started to speed up just from inhaling the incredible aroma of the roasting beans. Carlo's son, John, showed me how the beans are roasted, one variety at a time (they're not blended until after they're roasted because different beans roast for different amounts of time) in a towering chrome and red enamel roaster that looks like a cross between an espresso machine and a gleaming Italian fire truck. It's heated by a blazing oak wood fire, and the beans are carefully monitored for color and aroma to determine exactly when the roasting is done.

Then the blending begins. Mr. Espresso makes all kinds of great blends, but their most famous is Neapolitan, a secret mixture of eight to ten different beans from Indonesia, Latin America, and Africa blended in the style of Naples, where Carlo was born and raised.

As we chatted over a cup of smooth, creamy espresso, Carlo and John had fun deflating some of the common espresso myths. Espresso is a very dark-roasted coffee, right? Wrong! It's actually a medium roast. Too dark and it tastes bitter. Is it a sin to adulterate espresso with sugar? Ma non è vero! Nearly all Italians add sugar to their espresso. And I'll bet you think of espresso as super-caffeinated. Wrong again! A properly made espresso leaves most

AND FINALLY

A bee-filled super, a section of a bee hive, at Beekman Apiaries in Hughson, California.

of the caffeine in the grounds and has one- to two-thirds the caffeine of an 8-ounce cup of regular coffee.

Carlo and John are on a campaign to win the world over to the joys of espresso. They've certainly got my vote. I left with a whole new appreciation of my favorite bean.

A week later, I found myself surrounded by beans of a different kind—cocoa beans—at the Scharffen Berger Chocolate Factory in South San Francisco. Remember, we're in Northern California, so this isn't just any chocolate factory. A few years ago, the founders, John Scharffenberger and Robert Steinberg, set their sights on producing chocolates that rival the finest in the world. And they're already succeeding.

After years in the wine business, John applies many of the disciplines of winemaking to the craft of blending cocoa beans. Like Carlo's coffees, Scharffen Berger chocolates are blended from beans from all over the world—from Trinidad and Jamaica to New Guinea, Bahia, Venezuela, and Ghana. I watched as John and Robert split open dozens of raw beans and smelled and tasted them with the intensity of master sommeliers. As with coffee, the varieties are roasted separately. After roasting the beans for 30 to 40 minutes, Robert begins tasting them for doneness. I tasted a few beans

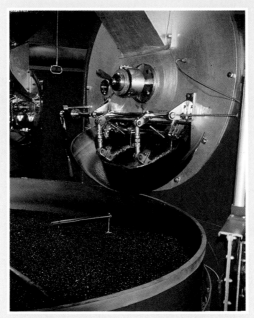

straight from the roaster and was surprised by how fruity and sweet they tasted, with a subtle hint of citrus flavor. Next, the beans are shelled in a winnower, leaving behind the nib—the kernel of the bean that will be turned into chocolate.

Robert's eyes lit up as he showed me the next step in the process: the mélangeur or mixer, in which the nibs are ground by heavy stone wheels over a heated surface, extracting the cocoa butter and creating a smooth paste, to which Madagascar vanilla beans and sugar are added. This is the magic moment. What had been a bin full of roasted beans is transformed before your eyes into a vat of warm, fragrant, glistening chocolate.

The chocolate gets refined and smoothed out in another machine called a concher, then tempered—heated and cooled to precise temperatures—to give it a beautiful glossy sheen and a mouth-melting texture. Finally, the warm, dark liquid chocolate is poured into molds and cooled.

On the following pages, you'll find all kinds of wonderful ways to finish off a meal. But if you're short on time, or just feel like keeping things simple, give yourself a break. As my visits to Mr. Espresso and Scharffen Berger reminded me, sometimes a great cup of coffee and some really delicious chocolate are the sweetest ending of all.

Freshly roasted coffee beans at Mr. Espresso,
Oakland, California.

After-Dinner Lemon Freeze

1 PINT (16 OZ/450G) VANILLA ICE CREAM, PREFERABLY HOMEMADE,
   SOFTENED AT ROOM TEMPERATURE FOR 20 MINUTES
7 TABLESPOONS (3$\frac{1}{2}$ FL OZ/80ML) LEMON JUICE
$\frac{1}{3}$ CUP (2$\frac{1}{2}$ FL OZ/75ML) VODKA

In a blender, mix the ice cream, lemon juice, and vodka
until it is smooth and pourable, 30 to 60 seconds.
Pour into glasses and serve immediately.

SERVES 6

Sgroppino is the name in Italian. It's tough to pronounce, but it's the most satisfying after-dinner drink imaginable. I had it a few years ago, sitting alongside the Mincio River outside of Verona. And then I didn't see it again until just last year when I was describing it to my waiter. Italians have this funny way of looking as if they've never before heard of such a thing—as if you are crazy! And then, they seem to remember. While it was still fresh in his mind, luckily for me, I got the recipe from him. Now I make it all the time and serve it in place of dessert.

Limoncello

15 LEMONS
2 BOTTLES 100 PROOF VODKA, 750 ML EACH
3¼ CUPS (21 OZ/630G) SUGAR

Peel the lemons with a vegetable peeler, avoiding the white pith from the back of the peel. Place the lemon peels in a large glass jar with 1 bottle of the vodka. Cover and place in a dark place for 40 days.

After 40 days, bring the sugar and 5 cups (40 fl oz/1.1 L) of water to a boil. Simmer for 5 minutes. Let the sugar syrup cool completely, then add it to the jar with the remaining 1 bottle vodka. Mix well, cover, and place in a dark place for 40 days.

After 40 days, strain and store 1 bottle at a time in freezer until ready to use. Serve directly from the freezer in chilled glasses.

MAKES ABOUT 4 BOTTLES, 750ML EACH

Opposite: Three refreshing lemon drinks: Limoncello, After-Dinner Lemon Freeze (page 189), and Lemon Verbena Elixir (page 192).

Lemon Jello?

WHEN I WAS LAST IN SORRENTO, ON THE ITALIAN Amalfi Coast just a skip south of Naples, a friend invited me to meet Concetta. "She's the best cook in town," she said. Concetta is an eighty-one-year-old woman who has lived all of her days in this pocket of paradise.

The day my friend and I arrived was a hot, humid summer day, when only the Mediterranean breezes bring relief. We sat on the terrace and Concetta brought us what looked like miniature martini glasses, all frosty and beaded with cold. From the freezer, she also brought a bottle of lemon-yellow liqueur. One sip of limoncello led to another, and to an afternoon I will not soon forget.

Limoncello is a digestif made only in Italy along the Amalfi Coast and on the islands of Ischia and Capri. It is pronounced *lee-moan-chello,* the last part like the musical instrument. When I first heard the word, I thought Concetta was saying "lemon jello." What kind of treat would this be? But after an afternoon of sitting gazing at the azure Mediterranean and sipping this liquid gold, I knew I had come across something special.

When I asked Concetta for the recipe, you would have thought I was asking for her first-born child. Much later, Concetta came from the kitchen with a small piece of white paper. She held tight to the recipe as she handed it to me and I tugged from the other side. All the time we were smiling, but finally I won the battle.

To make such a delectable drink is actually a very simple process, she revealed. It doesn't require much elbow grease, just a good bit of patience and some waiting time. But along the Amalfi Coast, time is what they have.

Lemon Verbena Elixir

3 PACKED CUPS (5 OZ/150G) LEMON VERBENA LEAVES
2 BOTTLES 100 PROOF VODKA, 750 ML EACH
3 CUPS (20 OZ/600G) SUGAR

*O*ne of my greatest inspirations is the Saturday farmer's market in San Francisco, where stall after stall offers some of the finest produce, breads, fresh fish, meats, sausages, cheeses, herbs, and flowers anywhere. One grower there, Joe Minoci, offers particularly interesting, esoteric herbs, greens, and vegetables. When I ran my fingers against his long, thin-leafed lemon verbena, it reminded me first of the teas, or tisanes, made in Provence. Next I was reminded of the elixirs made in France and Italy. What about using it to make an icy cold digestif? I tried it and fell in love with the results. Could this be the next limoncello?

Place the lemon verbena leaves in a large jar with 1 bottle of vodka. Cover and place in a dark place for 5 days.

After 5 days, bring the sugar and 4 cups (32 fl oz/900ml) of water to a boil. Simmer for 5 minutes. Let the sugar syrup cool completely, then add it to the jar with the remaining 1 bottle of vodka. Mix well, cover, and place in a dark place for 5 days.

After 5 days, strain and store 1 bottle at a time in the freezer until ready to use. Serve directly from the freezer in chilled glasses.

MAKES ABOUT 4 BOTTLES, 750ML EACH

Over-the-Top Wintermint Chocolate Cookies

4 OUNCES (120G) BITTERSWEET CHOCOLATE

12 OUNCES (350G) SEMISWEET CHOCOLATE

4 TABLESPOONS (2 OZ/60G) UNSALTED BUTTER

3/4 CUP (3 OZ/90G) ALL-PURPOSE FLOUR

1/2 TEASPOON BAKING POWDER

1/4 TEASPOON SALT

4 EGGS

1 CUP (6 1/2 OZ/200G) SUGAR

1 TABLESPOON PURE MINT EXTRACT

12 OUNCES (350G) SEMISWEET MINI-CHOCOLATE CHIPS

1/2 CUP (2 1/2 OZ/75G) CHOPPED WALNUTS, TOASTED (SEE PAGE 78)

Melt the bittersweet chocolate, semisweet chocolate, and butter together in a double boiler. Let cool for 10 minutes. In a bowl, combine the flour, baking powder, and salt.

Beat the eggs with the sugar until they form a stiff ribbon. Add the melted chocolate mixture to the eggs. Sift the dry ingredients on top and fold into the mixture along with the mint extract, mini-chocolate chips, and walnuts. Place the dough in the refrigerator and chill for 2 hours. When the dough is firm, remove from the refrigerator and divide into four logs, 1 1/2 inches (4cm) in diameter and 6 to 8 inches (15 to 20cm) long. Wrap each log in plastic wrap and refrigerate until cold and firm.

Preheat the oven to 350°F (175°C). Slice the dough into 1/4-inch (0.6-cm) slices and bake on an oiled or parchment-lined baking sheet until soft to the touch in the center but slightly firm on the edges, 7 to 9 minutes. Remove from the baking sheets immediately and cool on racks.

MAKES 5 DOZEN COOKIES

I'm not one who dies for a chocolate dessert, but I can't lie. When a chocolate dessert or cookie is set in front of me, I don't push it away. If you love chocolate, these cookies might become the bane of your existence. Make them ahead of time, store the raw dough wrapped in plastic in the freezer, and when you want them, simply slice off what you need and bake. It's a tempting proposition!

Pucker-up Citrus Crisps

1 CUP (6 $^{1}/_{2}$ OZ/200 G) SUGAR
$^{1}/_{4}$ CUP (2 FL OZ/60ML) LEMON JUICE
4 TABLESPOONS (2 OZ/60G) UNSALTED BUTTER, AT ROOM TEMPERATURE
2 TABLESPOONS HEAVY CREAM
$^{1}/_{2}$ TEASPOON LEMON OIL
1 TABLESPOON GRATED LEMON ZEST
$^{1}/_{2}$ TEASPOON BAKING SODA
1 CUP (3 $^{1}/_{2}$ OZ/100G) CAKE FLOUR
1 CUP (4 $^{1}/_{2}$ OZ/140G) TOASTED AND GROUND WHOLE ALMONDS WITH SKINS

I f you love lemon as I do, you're in for a treat. You will certainly see why I called these "pucker-up" citrus crisps. Enjoy these crisp cookies with raspberry lemonade or blueberry sorbet. Thanks to Julie Rethmeyer for her help with this recipe.

In a small saucepan, dissolve $^{1}/_{4}$ cup (1 $^{1}/_{2}$ oz/40 g) of the sugar in the lemon juice over medium heat. Simmer until it thickens slightly, about 1 minute. Add the butter, stirring just until melted. Remove from the heat and transfer the mixture to a bowl. Add the cream, lemon oil, remaining $^{3}/_{4}$ cup (4 $^{1}/_{2}$ oz/150g) sugar, lemon zest, baking soda, flour, and almonds and mix well. Refrigerate for 1 hour, until well chilled.

Preheat the oven to 350°F (175°C).

On a lightly floured surface, roll out the dough $^{1}/_{8}$-inch (0.3-cm) thick. Cut into strips, 1 $^{1}/_{2}$-inches (4-cm) wide. Cut 1 $^{1}/_{2}$-inch (4-cm) –wide strips on the diagonal in the opposite direction, to make diamond shapes. Transfer the crisps to a baking parchment-lined baking sheet and bake until lightly golden on the edges, 8 to 10 minutes. While baking, the crisps will puff and crack slightly. Remove from the pan and cool on a rack before serving. When they are cool, they will be crisp.

MAKES 3 TO 4 DOZEN

Coffee Hazelnut Biscotti

1 CUP (5 OZ/150G) HAZELNUTS

1 CUP (5 OZ/150G) WHOLE COFFEE BEANS, PREFERABLY
   FRENCH OR ITALIAN ROAST

$^1/_3$ CUP ($2^1/_2$ FL OZ/75ML) HEAVY CREAM

1 CUP PLUS 3 TABLESPOONS ($7^1/_2$ OZ/230G) SUGAR

8 TABLESPOONS (4 OZ/120G) UNSALTED BUTTER

2 EGGS PLUS 1 EGG YOLK

1 TABLESPOON COFFEE LIQUEUR, PREFERABLY TIA MARIA OR KAHLÚA

1 TABLESPOON PLUS 1 TEASPOON INSTANT COFFEE POWDER,
   DISSOLVED IN 1 TABLESPOON HOT WATER

3 CUPS (12 OZ/350G) ALL-PURPOSE FLOUR

1 TABLESPOON COCOA POWDER

1 TEASPOON BAKING POWDER

$^1/_2$ TEASPOON BAKING SODA

$^1/_4$ TEASPOON SALT

Biscotti is an Italian word that means "twice cooked." That is, you bake the cookies in a loaf shape first, then rebake them after they've been sliced. These dry crunchy morsels, rich with coffee and hazelnuts, are perfect for dunking into a café latte or with rich, creamy homemade vanilla bean ice cream. Make lots of these because you can store them in an airtight container for several weeks.

Preheat the oven to 350°F (175°C). Place the hazelnuts on a baking sheet and bake until golden brown and fragrant, 10 to 12 minutes. Allow them to cool for 2 minutes and then rub them briskly in a kitchen towel to remove as much of the skin as possible. Chop the hazelnuts into $^1/_4$-inch (0.6-cm) pieces and set aside.

To make a glaze, bring the coffee beans, cream, and 3 tablespoons (1 oz/30 g) of the sugar to a boil in a small saucepan over medium-high heat. Remove from the heat and let steep 1 hour.

Cream the butter and remaining 1 cup (6 $^1/_2$ oz/200 g) sugar together until light and fluffy. Add the eggs and egg yolk, one at a time, beating well after each addition. Add the coffee liqueur and instant coffee mixture. Sift together the flour, cocoa powder, baking powder, baking soda, and salt. Add the flour mixture in thirds, folding in the last third by hand with the hazelnuts. Chill the dough for 1 hour.

Divide the dough into 2 pieces and roll each into a log 3 x 10 inches (7.5 x 25 cm). Flatten each slightly. Place on a parchment-lined baking sheet. Strain the coffee beans from the cream and discard the beans. Brush the tops of the biscotti with the glaze and bake until a toothpick inserted into the center comes out clean, about 30 minutes. After the biscotti have been taken from the oven, brush the biscotti again with the glaze. While the biscotti are warm, slice them on the bias into $^1/_2$-inch (1.25-cm) slices.

Reduce the oven temperature to 300°F (150°C). Place the biscotti on a baking sheet, cut-side down, and bake about 10 minutes. Turn the biscotti and continue to bake until dry, 10 minutes more.

MAKES 3 DOZEN

Warm Chocolate-Walnut Tart

1 SHORT CRUST TART SHELL, PRE-BAKED (SEE INSTRUCTIONS FOR LEMON CLOUD TART, PAGE 176)

4 TABLESPOONS (2 OZ/60G) UNSALTED BUTTER, CUT INTO 8 PIECES

5 OUNCES (150G) BITTERSWEET CHOCOLATE, CHOPPED

1 CUP (8 FL OZ/240ML) DARK CORN SYRUP

$1/_4$ CUP ($1^1/_2$ OZ/45G) SUGAR

3 EGGS

2 TABLESPOONS BRANDY OR COGNAC

2 CUPS (10 OZ/300G) WALNUT HALVES, TOASTED (SEE PAGE 78)

1 CUP (8 FL OZ/240ML) HEAVY CREAM

2 TABLESPOONS ($2/_3$ OZ/20G) CONFECTIONERS' SUGAR

$1/_4$ TEASPOON VANILLA EXTRACT

Preheat the oven to 350°F (175°C). Make the dough, place it in a 9-inch (23-cm) tart pan, and prebake according to directions on page 176.

In a bowl set over a pan of simmering water, melt the butter and chocolate, stirring until smooth. Remove from the pan and place in a large bowl. In another saucepan over medium-high heat, stir together the corn syrup and sugar until boiling. Add to the chocolate. In a bowl, whisk the eggs and brandy or Cognac together until foamy and add to the chocolate mixture along with the walnuts. Stir well. Pour into the prebaked tart shell and bake until a skewer comes out of the center clean, 35 to 40 minutes.

Remove the tart from the oven and let cool 15 to 20 minutes, until warm. In the meantime, whip the cream to soft peaks and flavor with 1 tablespoon confectioners' sugar and the vanilla.

Cut the tart into wedges, dust the top with the remaining 1 tablespoon confectioners' sugar, and serve with the soft cream.

MAKES 1 TART, 9 INCHES IN DIAMETER, AND SERVES 8 TO 10

One of my closest friends adores chocolate and thinks the desserts that I like—sorbets, custards, and fruit tarts—are not really desserts at all. I'm sure you understand her sentiment if you ever get that craving for something rich and chocolaty. The texture of this tart is chewy, almost like a pecan pie, but with walnuts and lots of bittersweet chocolate instead of pecans. Enjoy with a big glass of ice-cold milk!

Coffee Honey Brulée

1$\frac{1}{2}$ CUPS (12 FL OZ/350ML) HEAVY CREAM

2 CUPS (16 FL OZ/475ML) WHOLE MILK

$\frac{3}{4}$ CUP (3$\frac{1}{2}$ OZ/100G) ITALIAN OR FRENCH ROAST COFFEE BEANS,
  COARSELY CRACKED

9 EGG YOLKS

$\frac{3}{4}$ CUP (6 FL OZ/180ML) HONEY

1 TEASPOON VANILLA EXTRACT

$\frac{1}{4}$ CUP (1$\frac{1}{2}$ OZ/45G) SUGAR

In a saucepan over medium heat, warm the cream, milk, and coffee beans. Remove from the heat and let sit for 2 hours.

Preheat the oven to 325°F (160°C). Strain the cream and milk through a fine-mesh strainer lined with cheesecloth or a paper towel. Discard the coffee beans. In a bowl, whisk together the cream and milk and egg yolks until blended. Whisk in the honey and vanilla. Divide the mixture evenly among 6 custard cups or ramekins, about 5 to 6 ounce (150 to 180ml) capacity. Place the custard cups in a baking pan and fill the pan with boiling water to reach halfway up the sides of the cups. Bake until a knife or skewer inserted into the center of the custard comes out clean, 45 to 55 minutes. Remove the cups from the baking pan and cool on racks for at least 1 hour.

Preheat the broiler. Before serving, sprinkle the sugar evenly over the tops of the custards. Place on a baking sheet and place them 2 to 3 inches (5 to 7.5 cm) from the heat source of a broiler. Broil until the sugar melts and caramelizes. Serve at room temperature.

SERVES 6

Hey honey, I know you're as busy as a bee but did you know that honeybees tap two million flowers to make one pound of honey?

When it comes to cooking with honey, the tables have certainly turned. Once relegated only to tea time, honey has moved from the back of the cupboard to great desserts like this one.

Espresso Truffle Ice Cream

1 CUP (5 OZ/150G) ESPRESSO ROAST COFFEE BEANS, COARSELY CRACKED

2 CUPS (16 FL OZ/475ML) WHOLE MILK

2¹/₂ CUPS (20 FL OZ/600ML) HEAVY CREAM

³/₄ CUP (5 OZ/150G) SUGAR

9 EGG YOLKS

3 TABLESPOONS (1¹/₂ FL OZ/45ML) COFFEE LIQUEUR,
   SUCH AS KALHÚA OR TÍA MARIA

4 OUNCES (120G) BITTERSWEET CHOCOLATE

1 OUNCE (30G) UNSWEETENED CHOCOLATE

5 TABLESPOONS (2¹/₂ OZ/75G) UNSALTED BUTTER

Place the coffee beans, milk, 2 cups (16 fl oz/475ml) of the heavy cream, and sugar in a large saucepan over medium heat. Stir until the sugar is dissolved. Remove from the heat and let steep for 1 hour. Strain the mixture through a fine mesh strainer lined with cheesecloth or paper towels.

In another saucepan, beat the egg yolks together. Reheat the cream to scalding. Pour about one-fourth of the hot cream into the egg yolks, whisking constantly. Add the rest of the cream, a little at a time, whisking constantly. Place the pan over low heat, stirring constantly with a flat-bottomed wooden spoon, and cook the mixture until it thickens enough to coat the back of the spoon, no hotter than 170°F (76°C). Immediately strain the mixture through a fine-mesh strainer into a bowl. Whisk for a minute to cool the mixture slightly. Add 2 tablespoons of the coffee liqueur and chill in the refrigerator until cold.

In the meantime, make the truffles. Melt the 2 types of chocolate, butter, and the remaining ¹/₂ cup (4 fl oz/120ml) cream in a small saucepan over low heat or over hot water, stirring constantly. Add the remaining 1 tablespoon coffee liqueur. Pour into an 8-inch (20-cm) pie plate or soufflé dish. Chill in the refrigerator until cold. When the chocolate is cold but still malleable, shape small truffles by dipping a half-teaspoon measuring spoon or a small melon-baller into hot water and quickly scooping a truffle. Lay the truffles on a sheet pan in a single layer, making sure that they do not touch one another. When you have shaped them all, chill them in the freezer until firm, about 1 hour.

Freeze the ice cream according to the instructions for your ice cream maker. Fold the chilled truffles into the ice cream during the last 2 minutes of churning.

MAKES ABOUT 1¹/₂ QUARTS (1.4L)

As a kid, I always ordered chocolate-chip ice cream. It was something about the little chocolaty bits, a kind of extra bonus. When I came upon this idea of folding tiny chocolate truffles into ice cream, I tried it with just about every flavor imaginable—mint, maraschino, lemon, vanilla, raspberry, even chocolate!

Warm Little Chocolate Cakes with Soft Centers

FOR THE CUSTARD SAUCE
1 1/2 CUPS (12 FL OZ/350ML) WHOLE MILK
3 TABLESPOONS (1 1/4 OZ/40G) SUGAR
1/2 VANILLA BEAN, SPLIT AND SCRAPED
3 EGG YOLKS

FOR THE CAKES
9 OUNCES (260G) BITTERSWEET CHOCOLATE, FINELY CHOPPED
6 TABLESPOONS (3 OZ/90G) UNSALTED BUTTER
2 TABLESPOONS COGNAC OR BRANDY
1/3 CUP (2 1/2 OZ/75G) SUGAR
4 EGGS, SEPARATED
3 TABLESPOONS (3/4 OZ/20G) CAKE FLOUR
CONFECTIONERS' SUGAR
FRESH RASPBERRIES OR CURRANTS AS A GARNISH

There is a restaurant in the Napa Valley that I love just because they serve these warm individual chocolate cakes. As you cut into them, the warm fudgy center oozes out and combines with a creamy vanilla custard sauce.

In a saucepan over medium heat, warm the milk, sugar, and vanilla bean, stirring constantly to dissolve the sugar. In a small bowl, whisk the egg yolks to break them up, but don't make them foam. Whisk a little of the hot milk into the egg yolks to warm them. Return the eggs to the pan and cook the custard, stirring constantly, until it coats the back of a spoon and reaches approximately 170°F (76°C). Test it by drawing your finger across the back of the spoon. If your finger leaves a trail in the custard, the custard has cooked to the right point. Immediately strain into a bowl and chill.

For the cakes, preheat the oven to 400°F (200°C). Butter and flour 6 ramekins, 5 to 6 ounces (150 to 180g) each. In the top of a double boiler, over medium heat, melt the chocolate, butter, and Cognac or brandy and stir until smooth. Set aside.

In a bowl, beat the sugar and egg yolks until ribboned and light colored. In another bowl, beat the egg whites until stiff. Gently fold the egg whites into the egg yolk mixture. Sift the flour over the top and fold the flour and chocolate into the egg mixture. Spoon the mixture into the prepared ramekins, distributing evenly. Place the ramekins on a baking sheet and bake until the cakes have risen and the tops just begin to crack, 10 to 12 minutes.

Immediately remove the ramekins from the oven and run a knife around the edges of the ramekins. Gently invert the ramekins onto 6 dessert plates. Spoon the sauce around the edges and dust the tops with confectioners' sugar. Garnish with raspberries or currants and serve warm.

SERVES 6

Index